Praise for

GiVE THEM JESUS

"Teaching children the Christian faith has never been more urgent than it is today. Parents need guidance and support as they seek to communicate with a generation exposed to influences coming from everywhere. Here is a book that speaks to these young people. It is a resource that every parent needs."

—Gerald Bray, research professor, Beeson Divinity School

"Raising up our children to know and love the Lord is our most important calling as Christian parents. But that important calling does not need to be complicated. Dillon Thornton gives us a wonderfully simple template by using the Apostles' Creed. I can't wait to see how God uses this book to build the faith of the next generation."

—Collin Hansen, editorial director of The Gospel Coalition and editor of *Our Secular Age* and *The New City Catechism Devotional*

"Solid doctrine. Clear writing. Extremely practical. Dillon Thornton's new book, *Give Them Jesus: Raising Our Children on the Core Truths of the Christian Faith*, is a must read for parents and grandparents who want to educate their children theologically, thus giving them an essential Christian education with a clear and keen understanding of the Gospel's basic core truths. This volume will help parents and grandparents to teach their children 'to see the person and work of Jesus more clearly.' I highly recommend it!"

—Denise George, author of 31 books, including
Teach Your Children to Pray

"Moms and dads, this is a marvelous book! Not only engaging and practical but also substantive and theological, here is a clarion call for parents to assume the primary responsibility for training their children in the way of Jesus. Gracious in tone yet firm in conviction, Dr. Dillon Thornton practices what he preaches—he is a pastor-theologian as well as a parent-theologian. I highly recommend reading this for your own nourishment and then engaging your family with the truths so winsomely articulated in this book!"

—Todd Wilson, senior pastor, Calvary Memorial Church

"Nothing is more important, or challenging, than training up children in the way they should go: the way of Jesus Christ. Catechism is a lost art, and the best place to recover this classic Christian practice is the home. For parents who are at a loss where and how to start, *Give Them Jesus* is a Godsend. I train pastor-theologians for a living, but I love the idea of the parent-theologian. Thornton gives parents what they need to know in order to give Jesus to their children."

—Kevin J. Vanhoozer, research professor of systematic theology,
Trinity Evangelical Divinity School

GiVE
THEM
JESUS

GiVE
THEM
JESUS

Raising Our Children on the Core Truths
of the Christian Faith

DILLON T. THORNTON, PHD

Faith
Words

FaithWords
Hachette Book Group
1290 Avenue of the Americas, New York, NY 10104
faithwords.com
twitter.com/faithwords

First Edition: September 2018

FaithWords is a division of Hachette Book Group, Inc. The FaithWords name and logo are trademarks of Hachette Book Group, Inc.

The publisher is not responsible for websites (or their content) that are not owned by the publisher.

The Hachette Speakers Bureau provides a wide range of authors for speaking events. To find out more, go to www.hachettespeakersbureau.com or call (866) 376-6591.

Scripture quotations marked (NRSV) and any that are unmarked are from the New Revised Standard Version Bible, copyright © 1989 by National Council of the Churches of Christ in the United States of America. Used by permission. All rights reserved.

Scripture quotations marked (ESV) are from the ESV® Bible (The Holy Bible, English Standard Version®), copyright © 2001 by Crossway, a publishing ministry of Good News Publishers. Used by permission. All rights reserved.

Scripture quotations marked (NIV) are taken from the Holy Bible, New International Version®, NIV®. Copyright © 1973, 1978, 1984, 2011 by Biblica, Inc.™ Used by permission of Zondervan. All rights reserved worldwide. www.zondervan.com. The "NIV" and "New International Version" are trademarks registered in the United States Patent and Trademark Office by Biblica, Inc.™

Library of Congress Cataloging-in-Publication Data has been applied for.

ISBNs: 978-1-4789-2071-7 (trade paperback); 978-1-4789-2072-4 (ebook)

Printed in the United States of America

LSC-C

10 9 8 7 6 5 4 3 2 1

To Aidan Thomas and Cullen Timothy

*"I have no greater joy than this,
to hear that my children are walking in the truth."*

3 JOHN 4

GiVE
THEM
JESUS

Contents

Introduction 1

Don't Pass Your Children to the "Professionals" 1

Becoming a Parent-Theologian 5

Prioritizing Family Worship 8

Starting with the Apostles' Creed 14

Chapter 1. The Father

Theology and Pastries 19

Thinking Rightly About the Triune God 21

Focusing on the Father 28

The Creator and His Good Creation 34

Chapter 2. The Son's Identity and First Coming

What Scrooge and Schwarzenegger
   Have in Common 49

Of Apple Trees and Apples: Humanity's Sinfulness 52

The Son with No Beginning: Jesus' Deity 56

God with Meat: Jesus' Humanity 60

The Mission of the God-Man 65

Chapter 3. The Son's Death and Resurrection

*The Challenge of Explaining the Cross
to Our Children* 75

*The Event of the Crucifixion: What Happened
at Golgotha?* 77

*The Dilemma of Our Pardon: Why Can't
God Just Forgive Us?* 81

The Perfect Substitute: What Is the Meaning
of the Cross and the Empty Tomb? 85

"Look to Jesus" 91

Chapter 4. The Son's Present Ministry and Second Coming

The New Creation and the Shark Who Ate Me 103

*The Appearance and Disappearance of Jesus:
Understanding the Ascension* 105

The Uncertainty of Jesus' Reappearance 112

The Reality of Resurrection 118

Planet Heaven 122

Chapter 5. The Holy Spirit

Killing the Heavenly Buzz 135

He Who Is God 137

He Who Gives Life 140

He Who Guides and Empowers 147

Scratching Dragons, Talking to Statues 155

Chapter 6. The Church

Why We Can't Be "Done" with the Church 167

Four Essential Features of the People of God 170

*Three Questions to Ask of a Potential
    Church Home* 178

*Concluding and Beginning Again: We Never
    Outgrow Our Need for the Gospel* 187

Acknowledgments 197

Notes 199

Introduction

*The primary calling of the parent-theologian
is to train children-disciples.*

DON'T PASS YOUR CHILDREN TO THE "PROFESSIONALS"

My favorite thing about Walt Disney World is the monster-size smoked turkey legs. Meeting Mickey is cool, but you can't eat him, so he doesn't compare to the turkey legs, at least not in my book. I vacationed at Disney World only once when I was a child. My wife, Jamie, on the other hand, went dozens of times with her family. When Jamie and I got married, we adopted her family tradition and started visiting "the Happiest Place on Earth" about once every three years. Unlike some family traditions, this one I really like. In a word: more turkey legs. Over the years, Jamie and I have traveled to Disney World, Disneyland, and the next thing on our list is the Disney Cruise Line.

Not long ago I was doing some research on Disney cruises, trying to determine how many of our children we would need to sell in order to pay for the cruise. As I watched one of their promotional videos, I was surprised to discover that on board each vessel they have "specially trained Disney counselors" who take care of your kids while you have some fun of your own. To me, this sounded like a slightly politer way of saying, "Dump your kids on the Disney professionals so you can enjoy Captain Jack's rum hoard."

Overall, I like Disney, and I don't want to be unduly critical. But how is this a *family* vacation? One of my privileges as a husband and father of two young boys is planning our family vacations, drawing a blueprint that will ensure that this time away from our crazy busy schedules will be a time of rest, rejuvenation, enjoyment, and togetherness. This is my responsibility, my joy. And I wouldn't give it up for anything, not even for all the turkey legs in the Magic Kingdom. So thanks, Disney counselors, but no thanks.

Watching the Disney Cruise Line promotional video, it occurred to me that many Christian parents think of their pastor or children's director as the "specially trained [spiritual] counselor." Rather than passing on spiritual truths to their children, countless parents merely pass their children to the "professionals" at church. While participation in a Christ-exalting local church is crucial, parents—not pastors, children's directors, or Sunday school teachers—bear the primary responsibility for their child's spiritual development. Consider the words of Moses, spoken centuries ago to the families of Israel:

> *Hear, O Israel: The LORD is our God, the LORD alone. You shall love the LORD your God with all your heart, and with all your soul, and with all your might. Keep these words that I am commanding you today in your heart. Recite them to your children and talk about them when you are at home and when you are away, when you lie down and when you rise. Bind them as a sign on your hand, fix them as an emblem on your forehead, and write them on the doorposts of your house and on your gates.*[1]

We find no hint here, or anywhere else in the Bible, of the training of children being abdicated by parents in favor of "professionals." As a well-known advocate of family-driven faith, Voddie Baucham, puts it, "Discipleship and multi-generational faithfulness *begins and ends at home.*"[2] Or to put it another way, "The family is God's divinely appointed 'small-group' discipleship program."[3]

The fundamental presupposition of this book is that Christian parents/guardians are responsible for the spiritual development of the children under their care. I am convinced that most parents *feel* this responsibility, though they have not been adequately equipped to *fulfill* it. Many years ago when I served as a children's pastor, an important Barna study was published.[4] The study revealed that roughly nine out of ten parents of children under the age of thirteen believe they have the primary responsibility for training their children in the faith, but a majority of these parents don't spend any time during a typical week discussing spiritual truths with their children. "Parents are not so much *unwilling* to provide more substantive training," the Barna study concluded, "as they are *ill-equipped* to do such work." The research further indicated that many parents are not able to guide their children spiritually because they themselves do not have a firm grasp of the Christian faith. "When it comes to raising children to be spiritually mature, the old adage, 'you can't give what you don't have,' is pertinent for millions of families." This is where I hope this present work will be of some help. My goal is to guide you, parents and guardians, to a deeper understanding of the core truths of the historic Christian faith, and along the way to arm you with appropriate language, helpful illustrations, and relevant object lessons so that in the end you will be better prepared to pass these truths on to your children. In short, I want to help you become a parent-theologian.

BECOMING A PARENT-THEOLOGIAN

Tedd Tripp, president of Shepherding the Heart Ministries, says that every parent's greatest need is "to understand deep truths from the Bible."[5] In other words, every mom and dad needs to become a parent-theologian. When you hear the word "theologian," I imagine you picture an old dude with a bodacious beard dwelling in a dusty study surrounded by big books. Granted, theologians need their books, and we'll come back to this point momentarily. But the thought of the theologian as an intellectual devoted solely to reading the works of dead guys while caring nothing about the world of the living is completely ludicrous. What, then, is a theologian? My favorite definition comes from Kevin Vanhoozer: a theologian is "one who opens up the Scriptures to help people understand God, the world, and themselves."[6] Vanhoozer continues: "Because God is the maker of everything that is, visible and invisible, and because the good news of God's self-giving love concerns the whole world, there is not a square inch in the cosmos, not a single aspect of human existence, that does not somehow relate to God and the gospel."[7] Theologians "get" this, and they help others "get" it. Theologians care about doctrine.

"Doctrine," now there's another word that's lost its street cred. Doctrine is not dry or stodgy, nor is it the cause of all division in the church, as some would have us believe. No, doctrine refers to the deposit of Christ-centered truth entrusted to the church's care, yet it's far more than a body of knowledge. It's instruction that forms, informs, and transforms us into doers of truth, disciples who think, speak, and act the way Christ did.[8] In caring about doctrine, the aim of the parent-theologian is not simply to add to our children's stockpile of knowledge, but to cultivate children-disciples who are able to display Christ-likeness in every situation. The aim is to train our children to love the Lord their God with all their heart, soul, mind, and strength.[9]

To become parent-theologians, we need proper tools; we need a well-stocked library. I can think of at least three types of resources we would be wise to gather. First, we need to collect books that will excite our children about the church and its history. When my boys were very young, I started reading them *The Church History ABCs*, by Stephen Nichols and Ned Bustard.[10] Before I knew it, my older son, Aidan, had named his stuffed hippopotamus Augustine. Proud dad moment. We've also used the Christian Biographies for Young Readers series, published by Reformation Heritage. This excellent series introduces children to important people in the Christian tradition, such as Athanasius, Augustine, Martin Luther, and John Calvin. Second, we need to collect books that will help our children understand the Bible. We have an abundant supply of works written specifically for children, picture books designed to introduce them to the story of the Scriptures or to basic Christian theology. Honestly, some of these books are rubbish. But many of them are very good. All of them, it seems, have a fascination with sheep. What is it with children's books and sheep? Essential for every household is Sally Lloyd-Jones's *The Jesus Storybook Bible*. Another staple is David Helm's *The Big Picture Story Bible*. Third, we need to collect books that will help us, as parent-theologians, grow in our grasp of the faith and assist us in the task of expressing our beliefs in child-friendly ways. *Give Them Jesus* falls into this latter category. If you picked up this volume hoping for a children's book, a work with more pictures than words, I'm sorry to say: You're going to be disappointed. I've written this book for parents, not for children, because, well, I didn't see a need for another woolly work.

PRIORITIZING FAMILY WORSHIP

Let's return to our definition of a theologian. A theologian is "one who opens up the Scriptures to help people understand God, the world, and themselves." A theologian is one who cares about doctrine, that unique kind of teaching that instructs the head, orients the heart, and guides the hand.[11] Formative instruction occurs in the natural rhythm and activity of life. Every day is a string of teachable moments; we chisel our children into Christlike men and women as we walk the aisles of the grocery store with them, gather around the dinner table, ride down the road in the truck, or take a Sunday afternoon hike through the mountains. In a sense, we are always teaching our children. Our responses and even our silence teach. Our charity and our irritability teach. Children are spongelike creatures, soaking up everything around them. We should be mindful of this reality, recognizing that as parent-theologians we are never really "off duty." But this reality does not negate the need for more focused times of instruction within the context of family worship.[12] Perhaps family worship is a new concept for you. Or maybe you've tried it before but it didn't work as you'd hoped. Teaching our children can be difficult, not least because they have the attention span of a gnat on LSD. Take, for example, a recent conversation I had with my boys while driving home from school:

Me: Boys, pretty soon Daddy is going to Indiana for a conference. I'm gonna miss you.

Cullen: Are you going to be preaching to the Indians there?

Me: No, Cullen, *Indiana*, not Indians.

Aidan: Do they speak English in India?

Me: No, Aidan, *Indiana*, not India.

Cullen: Are you going to meet Indiana Jones?

Me: Never mind where I'm going. Just be good for Mommy.

Family worship is most effective when it is characterized by brevity and consistency and when it is participatory. Family worship isn't a full-on church service. There's no need for a detailed order of worship, no reason for parents to wear robes (unless you're pretending to be a Jedi), and no obligation to prepare a thirty-minute expository sermon on Leviticus. When your children are young, ten to fifteen minutes will suffice for all the elements that compose the family worship time. The next key is consistency; determine how many days of the week the family will gather for worship, and then pick a time of day that works for everyone. Breakfast, dinner, and bedtime have all worked well for our family over the years. Currently, we're gathering early in the morning at the breakfast table. But this certainly doesn't mean that we are "holier" than the family that prefers to worship just before lights-out. The timing doesn't matter. Just be consistent. Make family worship a priority. Every family I know is omni-occupied: school, sports, music lessons, church activities, birthday parties, and the list goes on. Saying yes to family worship probably will involve saying no to some other activity. But a little less time running track is a small price to pay for helping our children learn how to walk in the truth.

Effective family worship is also participatory. The teaching time should feel less like a parent-to-child lecture and more like a family discussion. To accomplish this, parents need to develop the art of asking questions. At the conclusion of each chapter of this book, you will find a Family Worship Guide, which includes a list of discussion questions to use when teaching your children. Feel free to add to the list. One of the things that will happen as you ask these questions is that your children will develop questions of their own. This is a good thing. We want the home to be a place of inquiry and discovery. We create such an environment by (1) giving our children permission to ask questions about God, the Bible, and living the Christ-honoring life, (2) validating our children's questions, (3) answering their questions with biblical precision, and (4) teaching them how to find answers to their own questions by searching the Scriptures.[13]

What are the essential elements of family worship? I suggest four: teach, treasure, sing, and pray. Let's think about these in the reverse direction. First, every family worship time should include prayer. Prayer, simply stated, is paying attention to God. God is always present in our lives, and when we pause to pray, for three hours or for three minutes, we are acknowledging his presence. Sometimes we thank the Lord for his grace and goodness to us. Sometimes we confess our sins to him. Sometimes we ask God to work in our lives or in someone else's life. But we are always acknowledging that he is present and powerful, that he is great and we are greatly in need of him. Second, family worship should include singing.

Hymns and songs express biblical truths in artistic, poetic, and memorable ways. "They make an appeal to the soul on the basis of the beauty of the gospel. The gospel is already a beautiful reality, but through the use of hymns we learn to hear and feel and thus sense more deeply the beauty of God."[14] If you're nonmusical (like me), don't be intimidated by singing. Be courageous, and lead your family in making a joyful noise to the Lord. Do a little shopping on Amazon and pick out a good hymnal to keep at home. We often use *The Trinity Hymnal*, but there are many good songbooks available. In the Family Worship Guide sections of this book, I've given you the titles of several great hymns of the faith to get you started. If you're unfamiliar with the hymns I've chosen, they are readily available online. One of the most exhaustive sites is hymnary.org, but a quick Google search will provide a number of helpful websites. If you're stranded on an island and don't have access to the Internet, you're in luck: I've been told that any hymn can be sung to the tune of the *Gilligan's Island* theme song.

Third, part of our family worship time should be devoted to treasuring God's Word. The Psalmist declares, "How can young people keep their way pure? By guarding it according to your word. With my whole heart I seek you; do not let me stray from your commandments. I treasure your word in my heart, so that I may not sin against you."[15] Treasuring the Word means reading it carefully, committing it to memory, and then meditating on it frequently, which will enable us to walk obediently. The Family Worship Guides also include a short list of key Scriptures for you and your children to begin treasuring together. Finally, in addition to reading and memorizing Scripture, parents should commit a portion of the family worship time to teaching doctrine. Here we need to return to the critical line from the Barna study I quoted earlier: "When it comes to raising children to be spiritually mature, the old adage, 'you can't give what you don't have,' is pertinent for millions of families." For us to teach the basic Christian doctrines to our children, we must have an understanding of these doctrines ourselves. Not long ago I was speaking at a conference, addressing the subject of teaching our children about God. During the question-and-answer time that followed my talk, an older gentleman raised his hand and inquired, "What is *the one main thing* you want your children to know about God?" "That's easy," I said. "That, in Jesus, we know God's love for us." More than anything else, I want my children to understand the gospel, the good news of all that the loving God has accomplished for sinners in the person and work of Jesus Christ. This is why I think the ideal starting point for my children and yours is the Apostles' Creed.[16]

STARTING WITH THE APOSTLES' CREED

Some readers, especially those with a more liturgical background, will already be very familiar with the Apostles' Creed. Others will have no idea what I'm talking about, so a few introductory comments are in order. The Apostles' Creed is the oldest and simplest creed of the Christian church. The Creed gets its name, not because it was written by one of the apostles, but because it contains the main tenets of the apostles' teaching; it weaves together the big truths of the Bible. By the fourth century, the Creed as we now know it had assumed a more or less fixed form:

> *I believe in God, the Father almighty, Creator of heaven and earth.*
>
> *I believe in Jesus Christ, his only Son, our Lord. He was conceived by the power of the Holy Spirit and born of the Virgin Mary.*
>
> *He suffered under Pontius Pilate, was crucified, died, and was buried. He descended to the dead. On the third day he rose again.*

*He ascended into heaven and is seated at the right hand of
the Father. He will come again to judge the living and
the dead.*

*I believe in the Holy Spirit, the holy catholic church, the
communion of saints, the forgiveness of sins, the resurrection of the body, and the life everlasting. Amen.*[17]

Historically, the Apostles' Creed was the affirmation of
faith used at baptism. Before a person was baptized, he or she
would recite the Creed as a way of saying, "This is what Christianity is all about. As a follower of Jesus Christ, this is what I
believe."

In the Preface to *Mere Christianity*, C. S. Lewis paints a
beautiful picture that is worth contemplating in this context.
All Christians, Lewis says, live in one giant house. The various
denominations are doors or rooms within this house. Baptists
have their room: it's full of water, but there's hardly any wine.
Presbyterians have their room: there are many "elders," and
even some who are "elect." Anglicans have a room: you never
have to worry about the clergy dressing down too much. Pente-
costals have their room: it's loud. Though we have our denom-
inational distinctions, the most important thing to remember is
that all those who affirm the Apostles' Creed live together in

this one house; we compose the one family of God. The Creed unites believers throughout the world and across the centuries.[18] This is my first justification for claiming that the Creed is the ideal starting point for our children: because it's not basic *Baptist* doctrine or basic *Pentecostal* doctrine, but basic *Christian* doctrine. It introduces our children to the core truths of the historic Christian faith.

The other reason I insist on beginning with the Apostles' Creed is that it presents these core truths as a simple yet profound story in which our families participate. Nothing captivates children like a good story, and the Creed is "a portable story, a short summary of the scriptural story line that we can carry with us everywhere we go."[19] By learning the Apostles' Creed, we not only carry the great gospel story with us, but also we are reminded of our place within this story. Every time we repeat the words "I believe," we confess that we are characters who have been drawn into the drama of redemption.[20] The Apostles' Creed helps us and our children understand that Christians are not just *story-tellers*, but also *story-dwellers*.

In the six chapters that follow, I will unpack the Apostles' Creed. Additionally, I will assist parents in the task of articulating these core truths in child-friendly ways. That is, I aim to do *a share of the work*. In each chapter, I will offer pointers on how best to phrase certain doctrines. I will provide illustrations I have used with my own children. At times, I will even discuss analogies that often are used with children, but are best avoided. But all of this is only a portion of the work. You, of course, know your own children far better than I do, and you will need to do the hard but necessary work of thinking about the doctrines expounded in this volume and developing ways of explaining them to your family. My final advice to parent-theologians is to read each chapter of this book carefully, prayerfully, and to spend however many days or weeks you feel you need to walk your children through each chapter's Family Worship Guide in a thorough fashion. We dedicate countless hours to helping our kids throw a mean curveball or figure out fractions. These are decent endeavors. But the primary calling of the parent-theologian is to train children-disciples, and therefore our greatest joy in life should not be seeing our children win athletic competitions, earn academic scholarships, or choose lucrative careers, but seeing them walk in the truth. My prayer is that this book will help you and your children become story-dwellers, truth-walkers.

1
The Father

I believe in God, the Father Almighty,
Creator of heaven and earth.

THEOLOGY AND PASTRIES

Recently I attempted to explain to my five-year-old son, Cullen, that God is distinct *from* creation, yet he is perpetually and intimately at work *within* creation. As I would soon find out, this is not an easy concept to comprehend for a child who wears Lightning McQueen underwear. Later that week, Cullen had an appointment at the dentist. When he's brave at the dentist, we generally reward him by taking him to his favorite donut shop, which, it just so happens, is located right in front of our dentist's office. Strategic on the dentist's part, I've always thought. Cullen loves donuts. Really, really loves them. The great theologian, Augustine of Hippo, once wrote that innocence is found

19

in the child's limbs, not in the child's mind.[1] A child would kill you for what he wants, if not for his feeble limbs, Augustine declared. Well, Cullen might not kill you, but he would certainly rob you and put your money to good use buying donuts. On this particular day, the grandparents took Cullen to get his delectable, post-dentist treat. He was just about to take that monstrous first bite when, suddenly, he paused, looked up with a petrified expression, and asked: "Is God *in this donut*?" The grandparents promptly replied, "Ask your daddy."

My two boys are inquisitive, and I'm guessing they are not unique in this respect. Your children and mine will have questions, questions about sin and salvation, good and evil, God and grasshoppers, theology and pastries. We can't know when these questions are coming, but of this we can be certain: every inquiry is an opportunity to "train children in the right way."[2] *Children of faith need the diet of doctrine, and in the home, parents are the preparers of truth*. This means that Christian guardians must first have a firm grasp of the core teachings of the historic Christian faith. They then need to develop ways of explaining these tenets to their children without inadvertently diluting or distorting the faith. We begin in this chapter with the doctrine of God. When we lead our children to the water so they can drink deeply of the greatness of God, there will be born within them a God thirst that can never be satisfied by any lesser stream.

THINKING RIGHTLY ABOUT THE TRIUNE GOD

One of my favorite twentieth-century writers is A. W. Tozer. Excluding the Scriptures, Tozer wrote what is probably the most influential sentence I have ever read: "What comes into our minds when we think about God is the most important thing about us."[3] He goes on:

> *The gravest question before the Church is always God Himself, and the most portentous fact about any man is not what he at a given time may say or do, but what he in his deep heart conceives God to be like. We tend by a secret law of the soul to move toward our mental image of God. This is true not only of the individual Christian, but of the company of Christians that composes the Church. Always the most revealing thing about the Church is her idea of God, just as her most significant message is what she says about Him or leaves unsaid, for her silence is often more eloquent than her speech.... Were we able to extract from any man a complete answer to the question, "What comes into your mind when*

you think about God?" we might predict with certainty the spiritual future of that man.[4]

I want to rephrase Tozer's assertion to increase the forcefulness of it for parents in particular: *The most important thing about your child is his or her idea of God.* This is a countercultural claim, I know. Parents today tend to value most whatever it is they think will take their children farthest in life. Even many Christian parents have been duped into worshiping the success-promising trinity of good looks, good grades, and athletic ability. Having a high batting average is not a bad thing. The point is that if my power-hitting sons don't understand the greatness of God, I have not done my duty as a parent-theologian. In the same way, those who help their daughters to victory in a multitude of beauty pageants but who neglect to teach them about the majesty of God have failed their little girls. The truth is that both batting cleanup and winning pageants pale in comparison to thinking rightly about God.

How, then, do we develop right thinking about God, both in ourselves and in our children? The French reformer John Calvin says that all people have some conception of God. The problem, according to Calvin, is that we do not "apprehend

God as he offers himself."[5] In other words, the issue is not that God is absent from our minds; the problem is that the God present in our gray matter is a made-up deity we have fashioned to suit our fancy. We are not free to invent our own ideas of God. Rather, our concept of God must correspond as nearly as possible to what God has revealed about himself.

This brings us to the Apostles' Creed. When the Creed opens with the statement "I believe in God," it means the God who reveals himself in the inspired Word, Holy Scripture, and supremely in the incarnate Word, Jesus Christ.[6] Man does not discover God; God reveals himself to man. God has *spoken to us* through the prophets and apostles, and he has *come to us* in the person of Christ. Thus, the Swiss theologian Karl Barth (pronounced *Bart*, like *Bart Simpson*) is correct when he explains that Christ does not appear in the second act of the Creed only. "The whole Creed refers to our knowledge of God in Jesus Christ."[7] Not only is the Creed *Christological* or *Christ-centered*, but also it is *trinitarian*. The Creed has three main parts. In each part, a member of the Trinity takes center stage: (1) "I believe in God, *the Father*"; (2) "I believe in *Jesus Christ*"; and (3) "I believe in *the Holy Spirit*." The God of whom the Creed speaks has a "Christian name": Father, Son, and Spirit. This notion requires careful consideration, for children's literature, sermons, and lessons comprise a hotbed of heretical teaching, and nowhere is this truer than when dealing with the doctrine of the Trinity.

From beginning to end, Scripture attests to *the oneness of God*. In the Pentateuch, we read: "Hear, O Israel: The LORD our God, the LORD is one."[8] Jesus quotes this Old Testament text when he is asked about the most important commandment: "The most important is, 'Hear, O Israel: The LORD our God, the LORD is one. And you shall love the LORD your God with all your heart and with all your soul and with all your mind and with all your strength.' "[9] The idea of the oneness of God reverberates in the Pauline Epistles: "Indeed, even though there may be so-called gods in heaven or on earth—as in fact there are many gods and many lords—yet for us there is one God."[10] The consistent witness of Scripture is that God is one.

Yet the Bible also insists on *the "threeness" of God*. That the Father is God is evident from the fact that we are told to pray to him: "Our Father in heaven, hallowed be your name. Your kingdom come. Your will be done, on earth as it is in heaven."[11] That the Son, too, is God is clear from numerous New Testament texts, such as when the writer of Titus speaks of "waiting for the blessed hope and the manifestation of the glory of our great God and Savior, Jesus Christ."[12] Finally, the divinity of the Holy Spirit is affirmed most clearly in Acts 5:3–4, where Peter tells Ananias that lying to the Spirit constitutes lying to God.[13] Thus we find in the Bible a dual declaration: (1) There is one God; (2) The Father is God, the Son is God, and the Spirit is God. Confused yet?

The early Christians were, too. Over the course of many centuries and numerous debates, the church formulated an explicit doctrine of the Trinity, the *"three-in-oneness" of God.* The crucial terms of triune thinking are (of course) three: unity, equality, and distinguishability.[14] The Christian God is one indivisible unity. Christianity does not have three gods, but one God who meets us in three persons, Father, Son, and Holy Spirit. By "person," Christian theology does not mean "human being." Rather, the best way to think of personhood is to say that being a person means having the ability to give and receive love. Each person of the Trinity is fully God. Subordination-ism sees the Father as superior and the Son and the Spirit as some sort of second-rank deities. Modalism claims that God has three modes of existence that are not simultaneous. God's mission at a given time determines which form (Father, Son, or

Spirit) he takes. On the contrary, the Christian teaching is that the persons of the Trinity are coequal and coeternal. Though equal, the persons are distinguishable; the Father is not the Son, the Son is not the Spirit, and so on. We may summarize the classical trinitarian teaching as follows.

> God eternally exists as three distinct persons:
>   Father, Son, and Spirit.
> Each person is fully God.
> There is one God.[15]

The triune reality of God is a mystery; Christians affirm the doctrine without fully understanding it. Our lack of complete comprehension shouldn't bother us. After all, a God small enough to be fully understood wouldn't be big enough to be worshiped. In an effort to help people, and especially children, better understand the doctrine of the Trinity, preachers and teachers have employed a wide range of analogies or comparisons. Parents would do well to avoid these. To suggest that God is like a three-leaf clover is inadequate, because each leaf is only part of the clover, and God has no parts; he is one indivisible unity. We run into the same problem when we liken God to an egg, which is composed of three parts: shell, white, and yoke. Comparing God to the three forms of water—steam, liquid, and ice—is also problematic, because no amount of water can be all three forms at once, so when we use this analogy, we end up with a house full of miniature modalists!

Though clovers fail, most children will find it helpful to have something to look at, so I suggest using the "shield of the Holy Trinity," a diagram found in medieval symbolism. An English version of the shield is provided below.[16]

Kids love shields. And this one is really useful, as it captures important concepts of triune thinking, such as equality

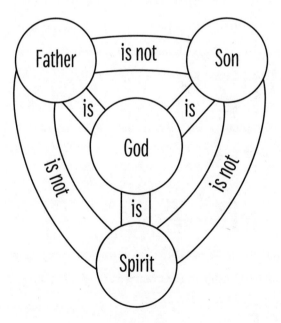

and distinguishability. But perhaps the best way to help our children *experience* the triune reality of God is to teach them to pray. As my literary hero, C. S. Lewis, says:

> *An ordinary simple Christian kneels down to say his prayers. He is trying to get in touch with God (the Father). But if he is a Christian he knows that what is prompting him to pray is also God (the Holy Spirit): God, so to speak, inside him. But he also knows that all his real knowledge of God comes through Christ, the Man who was God—that Christ is standing beside him, helping him to pray, praying for him. You see what is happening. God is the thing to which he is praying.... God is also the thing inside him which is pushing him on.... God is also the road or bridge along which he is being pushed.... [The triune reality of God is being experienced] in that ordinary little bedroom where an ordinary [boy] is saying his prayers.*[17]

FOCUSING ON THE FATHER

The Apostles' Creed begins by affirming the fatherhood of God. If we scour the Scriptures, we can identify three principal ways in which the term "Father" is used of God. First, the term

"Father" characterizes God as the one who generates all things. We will consider this point in detail momentarily. For now, suffice it to say that, when we speak of God as Father in this first sense, we are speaking of his creative power. The author of Ephesians writes, "I bow my knees before the Father, from whom every family in heaven and on earth takes its name."[18] God created every family, and he proclaims his lordship over each one by naming it. Similarly, the Psalmist says that God determines the total number of stars, and gives to all of them their names.[19] Precisely what the names are doesn't matter. The important thing to note is that the Father is the Creator of the universe, and he exercises authority over all he has made.

Second, the title "Father" is used more specifically of God as the loving and protective Father of believers. Any idea of God as an impersonal force—something akin to a nebula or a puff of smoke—is ruled out by the reference to God as Father. God is a personal being who cares deeply for us and who desires our good. In this respect, God is like a human father. We must, however, avoid thinking of God as being in the *form* of a human father. For as John Calvin reminds us, "God's glory is corrupted by an impious falsehood whenever any form is attached to him."[20] God cannot "fit" into any shape we can construct, and we insult him when we try to cram him in. One of the most amazing truths of Christianity is that it is *this infinite God* who enters into *a personal relationship* with believers. To receive Christ is to become a child of God. Surely this is the highest blessing of the gospel, to be taken into God's family and fellowship, to be established as his children and heirs.[21] As sons and daughters, we have the privilege of speaking with our Heavenly Father freely and without fear.[22] And he is a Father who knows how to give good gifts to his children.[23]

The fatherhood of God has to do not just with God's affection and provision, but also with his discipline of believers. The writer of Hebrews tells us that God "disciplines us for our good, in order that we may share his holiness."[24] Most people probably don't like the sound of this. Honestly, we prefer a geriatric deity kicked back in some corner of the cosmos, giggling at the lot of mischievous mortals. As C. S. Lewis puts it, "We want, in fact, not so much a Father in Heaven as a grandfather in heaven—a senile benevolence who, as they say, 'liked to see young people enjoying themselves,' and whose plan for the universe was simply that it might be truly said at the end of each day, 'a good time was had by all.'"[25] But our Heavenly Father is far too concerned with our holiness to sit idly by. "Discipline always seems painful rather than pleasant at the time, but later it yields the peaceful fruit of righteousness to those who have been trained by it."[26]

At this point, a concern should be mentioned. Men and women who have had abusive or absentee earthly fathers often find the idea of God as Father to be offensive. Certainly, we are experiencing a family crisis, at least in the West. Millions of American children now grow up without fathers in the home. Can the idea of the fatherhood of God be salvaged for these fatherless children? Indeed it can. In fact, it must be. One way to deal with this concern is to reverse the direction of the analogy: rather than thinking that God is like our earthly fathers, we should understand that earthly fathers are called to be as loving as God is.[27] Every earthly father is a son of Adam, which means that no flesh-and-blood father is perfect, and always there will be some who will severely mistreat their children. When faced with the failures of our earthly fathers, we must remember that the true definition of fatherhood is to be found in God. Those of us who have been brought into God's family have done nothing to earn our place there, and we can do nothing to merit our banishment. By grace we have been brought into the Father's loving arms. By grace we are kept in his tight embrace. We are protected, provided for, and even chastened by God, yet never cast off. We are sealed to the day of redemption; we will inherit the promises, as heirs of everlasting salvation.

Third, the title "Father" is used to explain to us the relationship between the first and the second persons of the Trinity: he is the Father of the unique Son, Jesus Christ. Here we must recall the classical doctrine of the Trinity, which was summarized above. In the New Testament, the Son submits to the Father, as in Luke 22:42 ("not *my* will but *yours* be done"), not because the Father is greater or somehow "more God," but simply because this is how the members of the Trinity relate to one another. Also in the New Testament, Christ is called the Father's "only begotten Son" and the "firstborn of all creation."[28] Taken in isolation, these verses seem to teach that the Son was the first of God's creatures. But such texts must be understood in the context of others that clearly teach the eternality of the Son. The Son was with the Father from the very beginning, and everything the Father made was made together with the Son.[29] Arianism, a fourth-century heresy, claimed of the Son, "There was a time when he was not." But orthodox Christianity claims, "There *was not* when he *was not*." The point of the "only begotten" and "firstborn" language is to showcase the Son as the *heir* to all things. As the heir, Christ shares the Father's authority over all creation.[30]

Having examined the three ways in which the term "Father" is used of God, we turn now to the next term of the Creed: "I believe in God, the Father *almighty*." The Bible tells us many things about God. He is eternal, unchanging, all-present, all-knowing, good, holy, just, loving, wise, and so on. In theological lingo, these are the "attributes" or "perfections" of God. The question "What is God?" is a question we cannot answer exhaustively, for the finite cannot fully comprehend the infinite. But the questions "What is God like?" and "How should we expect him to act toward us?" are questions that are answered by God's attributes. The attributes are not separate parts of a composite God. Put another way, God is not presliced; he bears no resemblance to the pizza my family just devoured. The attributes cannot be considered as parts of God, because, again, he is *one indivisible unity*. It is therefore never the case that the "part" of God that is loving is active toward us one day while the "part" of God that is just is active the next. God is *entirely* loving and *entirely* just, and he is so all the time. *Everything* God does is fully consistent with *every one* of his attributes.[31]

The divine attribute that surfaces most in Scripture is the one expressed in this opening part of the Apostles' Creed: God is "almighty." The term "almighty" refers to God's sovereignty, his all-pervading control. God's power is supreme over everyone and everything else, and he rules his creation directly. As the children's song says, "He's got the whole world in his hands." The term "almighty" is not, however, a declaration of God's ability to do any and all things. There is one important restriction on God's power, which Scripture pinpoints for us: "he cannot deny himself."[32] What this means is that God is able to do everything *that is consistent with his character.* God cannot use his power to act in evil, unjust, or unwise ways, because such things are inconsistent with his character. This is a remarkably comforting thought for those of us who belong to the Father almighty. God has committed himself to us, and the fact that he is almighty doesn't mean that he can or will change his mind about this.[33]

THE CREATOR AND HIS GOOD CREATION

The first part of the Creed concludes with an affirmation of God as the "Creator of heaven and earth." God is sovereign over all because he is the Creator of all. The Christian doctrine of creation may be stated in a memorable, child-friendly line: *Everything* was made by *the three-in-one Someone* who himself was made by *no one*. God himself knows neither beginning nor end. The Psalmist writes, "Before the mountains were brought forth, or ever you had formed the earth and the world, from everlasting to everlasting you are God."[34] God is the uncreated one or, more precisely, the uncreated three-in-one. Among the persons of the Trinity, there has been perfect communion and completion for all eternity; therefore, we cannot say that God created the world because he was lonely or somehow unfulfilled. God does not need humans, or any other part of his creation. "Need" is a creaturely word. Creation, then, is not an act of necessity, but of charity. To use once more the words of C. S. Lewis, "God, who needs nothing, *loves into existence* wholly superfluous creatures in order that He may love and perfect them."[35]

In the first chapter of Genesis, the loving work of creation is pictured as a language that only God can speak. "Once upon a time, everything was silent. There were no jazz clubs, infomercials, or thunderstorms. There were no barking dogs or honking horns. It was untamed tranquility."[36] Then, God *spoke*; and the universe *was*. Though the Father is in the foreground in the work of creation, Scripture indicates the involvement of the Son and the Holy Spirit. The Son is described as the one "through" whom creation came about.[37] The Spirit, like the Son, has been at work from the beginning, "hovering over the face of the waters," giving life to creatures.[38] To borrow a phrase from my older son's favorite flick, *The Lego Movie*, the triune God is the "master builder" of the cosmos. But unlike Emmet, who crafts things out of material already before him, God creates out of nothing. What scholars refer to as *creatio ex nihilo* ("creation out of nothing") is an important tenet of the Christian faith. If something other than God existed in the beginning, some maverick molecule, then God is not the *source* of all things, and thus is not *sovereign* over all things. Scripture teaches precisely what the Creed affirms: The eternal, uncreated God is the Creator of "heaven and earth," that is, *all things*, things great and small, high and low, visible and invisible. What this means is that pantheism, the belief that everything *is* God, is not so much false as it is hopelessly outdated. Once, before creation, it would have been correct to say that *everything* is God, because there was *nothing* except him.[39]

That the Scriptures begin with an account of the creation of the cosmos reveals that the question of origins is significant for Christian theology. In fact, so important are the teachings of the first chapters of the Bible that there were more commentaries written on Genesis 1–3 in the early centuries of the church than on any other section of Scripture. But we must admit that there are some things about which Genesis does *not* tell us. Aside from the central belief that the world in which we live was established by the action of God, Genesis 1–2 are not interested in telling us *how* things were created. Precisely how long it took God to create the world, and the means he chose to achieve his purpose, are questions Genesis does not answer. The issue with the duration of the creative action is that the word our English Bibles translate as "day" is the Hebrew word *yôm*, which can refer to periods of time longer than 24 hours. Some Christians choose to believe the world was created in six 24-hour days, which is fine. The problem arises when this view is treated as the only position the true believer may hold. Genesis leaves ample room for other theories. In my mind, the creation of the sun and the moon on the *fourth* day, not the *first*, makes it difficult to argue for six 24-hour days, since the concepts of evening and morning would be meaningless without the sun. We also make a mistake when we read Genesis 1–2 as if they were intended to compete with modern cosmological hypotheses, such as the big bang theory. Parents need not fear such theories being taught to their children in public schools, because these theories do not necessarily contradict the teaching of the Bible. It may be that the universe burst into being some 14 billion years ago. If so, Christian theology contends that it was God who lit the match, so to speak. In sum, Genesis 1–2 are not scientific descriptions, but poetic accounts, doxological declarations that direct our attention to the God who called the entire creation into existence.

The created world is "the most beautiful theater," the place where God's plan is played out.[40] In the *theodrama*, many characters take the stage, and each one has a purpose. We may not know why some creatures exist. What could possibly be the point of the Pomeranian? The mosquito? But whether we understand their purpose or not, all creatures matter, because they all originate with God and are able to give glory to their Creator. In their own ways, the star, the shrub, and the sloth lift up praises to God.[41] Within the community of creation, humans are unique. Humanity has been given "dominion" over the earth, a term that suggests a unique responsibility.[42] We must answer to God for the way we steward the resources he has supplied for us and his other creatures. Humans are also distinct in the created order in that we have been created in the "image" of God.[43] Men and women are created with the capacity to relate to God in ways other creatures cannot. We remain unsatisfied, unfulfilled, incomplete until we enter into a personal relationship with the one who made us.[44]

Evil is not part of God's creation. Genesis 1 affirms the fundamental goodness of everything God made. The existence of evil was the result of rebellion against God, rebellion made possible because God gave spiritual beings and humans the free will to disobey his commands. Disobedience first manifested itself among the angels. Satan, presumably a fallen angel, was permitted access to the first man and woman, Adam and Eve. They were deceived by him, sinned against God, and were therefore banished from God's presence.[45] All descendants of Adam and Eve inherit this broken relationship; in our natural state we are separated from God, slaves of Satan, sinners by condition and choice.[46] Whatever free will we possess, we can exercise only within the constraints of our sinful condition. An illustration that may prove helpful for children is this: We are free like fish in an aquarium are free.[47] We can do a thousand things, but the one thing we cannot do is escape from the confines in which we have been placed because of our first parents' sin. (Of course, if your children have seen *Finding Nemo*, then this analogy may be ruined, since in that movie the pesky little fish do manage to climb out of their aquarium!)

The doctrine of creation is not only about the God who made the world *in the beginning*; it is also about the God who is with us *in the now*. For starters, Scripture teaches that the

Creator remains present everywhere in his creation; God fills heaven and earth.[48] Unlike the pantheists I mentioned earlier, who propose that everything *is* God, Christians confess that God is present everywhere in creation, while maintaining that he is distinct from creation. Returning to my son's inquiry about the donut, I suppose it is right to say that God is present in pastries, because God *pervades* the oceans, the mountains, the trees, and all other parts of his world. But this does not mean that God is *enclosed* in any of these, because, as we have already learned, he is infinite. And it certainly does not mean that God *is* a glazed treat. To help children understand how God can be present within creation and yet distinct from creation, I suggest the object lesson of the sponge.[49] Fill a bucket with water and then wet the entire sponge. Next, explain to your children that, as the water is present everywhere in the sponge though different from the sponge, so God is present throughout his creation though distinct from it. You could further explain that the water inside the sponge is present but not visible. In the same way, God is always with us, even though we cannot see him with our eyes.

When the Bible tells us that God is present everywhere in creation, it does not mean that he merely sees everything that takes place within the theater of the universe. God is not a spectator, some passive observer. Rather, God is present every-where in creation and *at work in all things*. The Creator of all is also the everlasting Governor and Preserver; God sustains, nourishes, and cares for everything he has made. In the words of John Calvin, "Governing heaven and earth by his providence, [God] so regulates all things that *nothing takes place without his deliberation*."[50] Deism has no place for God in day-to-day life. For deists, God is the absentee landlord, the guy who rents us the flat (earth) and then disappears. To the contrary, Christians believe that God is intimately involved with his creation. The ultimate demonstration of God's continual involvement is the *incarnation*, the sending of the Son to deal with the corruption of God's good creation. This all-important subject is the focus of the next two chapters.

FAMILY WORSHIP GUIDE

The Apostles' Creed

As a family, memorize the first part of the Creed in three simple steps:

> *I believe in God,*
> *the Father Almighty,*
> *Creator of heaven and earth.*

Key Verses

In addition to memorizing the first line of the Creed, choose one or more of the following passages to treasure in your heart:

THE CREATOR/MASTER BUILDER

> *In the beginning God created the heavens and the earth.*
> *(Genesis 1:1 NIV)*

CREATED IN THE IMAGE OF GOD

> *So God created mankind in his own image, in the image*
> *of God he created them; male and female he created them.*
> *(Genesis 1:26–27 NIV)*

THE UNCREATED GOD

> *Lord, you have been our dwelling place throughout all generations. Before the mountains were born or you brought forth the whole world, from everlasting to everlasting you are God. (Psalm 90:1–2 NIV)*

CALLING ON OUR HEAVENLY FATHER

> *Ask and it will be given to you; seek and you will find; knock and the door will be opened to you. For everyone who asks receives; the one who seeks finds; and to the one who knocks, the door will be opened. (Matthew 7:7–8 NIV)*

THE FATHER'S SENDING OF THE SON

> *And we have seen and testify that the Father has sent his Son to be the Savior of the world. (1 John 4:14 NIV)*

Nuggets of Truth

Parent-theologians, when teaching your children-disciples, be sure to cover these main points from Chapter 1:

THINKING RIGHTLY ABOUT THE TRIUNE GOD

- The most important thing about us is what comes into our minds when we think about God.

- We are not free to invent our own ideas about God; rather, our concept of God must correspond as nearly as possible to what he has revealed about himself.

- God has revealed himself to us in the Scriptures and supremely in the person and work of Jesus Christ.

- The Bible teaches us about the *"three-in-oneness"* of God. The doctrine of the Trinity may be summarized as follows: God eternally exists as three distinct persons (Father, Son, and Holy Spirit); each person is fully God; and there is only one God.

FOCUSING ON THE FATHER

- In the Bible, we find three main ways in which the term "Father" is used in reference to God.

  ○ First, the term characterizes God as the one who creates all things.
  ○ Second, the title "Father" is used more specifically to refer to God as the loving and protective Father of believers. To receive Christ is to become a child of God.

- ° Third, the title "Father" is used to explain to us the relationship between the first and the second persons of the Trinity: he is the Father of the one-of-a-kind Son, Jesus Christ.
- The Bible tells us many things about God: he is eternal, unchanging, all-present, all-knowing, good, holy, just, loving, wise, etc. These are called the *attributes* or *perfections* of God. The attribute that surfaces most in Scripture is God's sovereignty, his complete control over his creation.

THE CREATOR AND HIS GOOD CREATION

- The Christian doctrine of creation may be stated simply: Everything was made by the three-in-one Someone who himself was made by no one.

- All creatures matter, because they all originate with God and are able to give glory to their Creator.

- Within the community of creation, humans are unique. We have been given *dominion* over the earth, which means that we must steward the resources God has supplied for us and his other creatures.

- We are also distinct in the created order in that we have been created *in the image of God*. Humans are created with the capacity to relate to God in ways other creatures cannot. We remain incomplete until we enter into a personal relationship with the one who made us.

- Evil is not part of God's creation. The existence of evil was the result of rebellion against God, rebellion made possible because God gave spiritual beings and humans the free will to disobey his commands.

- All descendants of Adam and Eve inherit a broken relationship with God; in our natural state we are separated from our Creator, slaves of Satan, sinners by condition and choice.

Questions for the Family

Use these questions to spark discussion during your family worship times:

THINKING RIGHTLY ABOUT THE TRIUNE GOD

- Where do we turn to learn the truth about God? Can you think of any misleading ideas about God communicated in books, movies, television shows, etc.?

- What does the term "Trinity" mean? Why is this doctrine so important?

FOCUSING ON THE FATHER

- What do we mean when we say that God is our Father?

- How does God show his fatherly love for us?

- What does the word "almighty" mean? How is the sovereignty (or special power) of God a comforting truth for us?

THE CREATOR AND HIS GOOD CREATION

- What are some of your favorite parts of God's creation?

- How do you think God wants us to treat his creation?

- How are people different from the rest of creation?

- If everything God created was good, how did sin and evil (or bad things) come into the world?

Songs That Celebrate These Truths

As you study the truths summarized in part one of the Creed, also celebrate these truths as a family. Sing the following songs together, and try to memorize at least the first verse of each one.

- "Holy, Holy, Holy"

- "All Creatures of Our God and King"

Prayer Prompts

Always conclude your family worship times with prayer. Here are some prayer themes to keep in mind while your family studies part one of the Creed:

- The role of Scripture in learning the truth about God

- The truth of one God in three persons: Father, Son, and Spirit

- The sovereignty or special power of God

- The beauty and goodness of God's creation

- The uniqueness of humans

2
The Son's Identity and First Coming

I believe in Jesus Christ, his only Son, our Lord.
He was conceived by the power of the Holy Spirit
and born of the Virgin Mary.

WHAT SCROOGE AND SCHWARZENEGGER HAVE IN COMMON

Several ways of approaching Christmas result in our missing the true meaning of the season entirely. One way is epitomized in that icy Dickens character, Ebenezer Scrooge. "Scrooge! a squeezing, wrenching, grasping, scraping, clutching, covetous old sinner! Hard and sharp as flint...solitary as an oyster. The cold within him froze his old features, nipped his pointed nose, shrivelled his cheek...made his eyes red, and his thin lips blue.... External heat and cold had little influence on Scrooge. No warmth could warm, nor wintry weather chill him." This is the opening description from the 1843 novella *A Christmas*

Carol. When Scrooge first speaks in the story, it's in response to his nephew, who has just wished him a Merry Christmas. "Humbug," Scrooge replies. "Merry Christmas! What right have you to be merry? What reason have you to be merry? You're poor enough.... What's Christmas time to you but a time for paying bills without money; a time for finding yourself a year older, and not an hour richer.... If I could work my will,...every idiot who goes about with 'Merry Christmas' on his lips should be boiled with his own pudding and buried with a stake of holly through his heart!"

Like Scrooge, some people camouflage Christmas rather than celebrating it; they attempt to drain everything unique and wonderful out of the season, doing their best to make it look like every other time of year. Christmas is merely another time for hard work, another opportunity to acquire fame and fortune.

A second approach is embodied in *Jingle All the Way*, the late 1990s Christmas comedy starring that masterful thespian Arnold Schwarzenegger. (Yes, I can move rather effortlessly from Dickens to Schwarzenegger. I'm an eclectic guy.) In the movie, the hottest new toy, out just in time for Christmas, is the Turbo Man action figure. The movie follows two fathers as they race through town in search of the last Turbo Man on the shelves. The implicit message of the movie is that Christmas will be ruined, and these fathers will be failures, if they don't buy the right gift. This way of thinking is more common in the Christian community than we care to admit. We've even justified it by bringing in bits of the Christmas story. The Wise Men brought gifts to Jesus, so surely there can be no Christmas without expensive presents. As Regional Manager Michael Scott from *The Office* puts it, "Presents are the best way to show someone how much you care. It's this tangible thing that you can point to and say, 'I love you this many dollars' worth.'"

On the surface, these two approaches seem very different. The first is characterized by greed. The second by what appears to be generosity, though actually it's a pseudo-generosity, insecurity disguised as openhandedness. Coming to this realization helps us see that there's a common denominator in these two approaches: the idea of *earning*. The Scrooge types work endlessly to obtain wealth, power, and prestige. The Turbo Man–hunting types shop tirelessly and overspend in an effort to gain the love of family or friends. After a hard day's work, both sorts proudly proclaim, "I've earned it." This is where the true message of Christmas enters the ring hitting harder than the

Russian from *Rocky IV*, which, it just so happens, is my favorite Christmas movie.

Christmas—and Christianity—is not about earning, working hard to get what we deserve. Rather, it's all about *grace*. It's about Jesus coming to earth to do everything necessary so that sinners can be forgiven, so that we can receive something far better than what we deserve. In this chapter we will explore the identity of Jesus and his arrival on the scene. But we must begin by attending to the question: Why did Jesus need to come to earth?

OF APPLE TREES AND APPLES: HUMANITY'S SINFULNESS

The first line of the Apostles' Creed left us at the doctrine of creation. In the beginning, God loved his creation into existence. Of all God's creatures, humans are distinct. Genesis teaches us that humans were created in the image of God, wired for intimate fellowship with the Creator. Such intimacy existed in the beginning, but it didn't last. A catastrophe of cosmic proportions occurred in Genesis 3. Adam and Eve turned away from God and followed the deceptive serpent. Adam's rebellion, just as God threatened, had "death" as its consequence.[1] By death, the Bible means not just physical death, but also spiritual death, separation from the loving and life-giving presence of God. After the events of Genesis 3, the peace and intimacy Adam and Eve once experienced with God was gone; their relationship with their Maker became one of conflict and hostility leading to condemnation.

This rebellion was not just headline news in the Garden of Eden; it's news for us today—bad news. Why? Because the name "Adam" means "man" or "mankind." As the first man, Adam served as a representative. God placed him in the Garden to act not simply for himself, but also for all of his future descendants. The Apostle Paul writes in Romans 5:18–19, "*One man's* trespass led to condemnation for *all*," and "By the *one man's* disobedience *the many* were made sinners." What Adam did in the Garden long ago affects my family today. It affects you and your children, too. Sinfulness marks each and every human being from birth. Elsewhere Paul says that we are sinners "by nature."[2] This is sometimes referred to as the doctrine of *original sin*. As descendants of Adam, we are sinful or corrupt to the very core of our being. Scripture never suggests that we are innocent until we commit our first sinful action. Remember what Augustine said: that baby in the crib would kill you for what he wants, if only he had the strength to do it.[3] Cute and cuddlesome little Johnny is innocent, all right, but only in his limbs. At his core, he's sinful, like all sons of Adam and daughters of Eve. Here's the way the great Anglican theologian J. I. Packer puts it: "The assertion of original sin makes the point that we are not sinners *because we sin*, but rather we sin *because we are sinners*, born with a nature enslaved to sin."[4]

How do we explain the concept of original sin to our children? I recommend taking a family field trip to an apple orchard (or just use your imagination). Ask your children, "Would you say that a tree bears apples because it already is an apple tree, or does the tree become an apple tree when it produces its first apple?"[5] It's pretty clear that a tree produces fruit according to its nature. When an apple tree is old enough, it bears apples. Likewise, as our children grow, they show themselves to be sinners. In time, they behave like their first human father.

The sinful nature manifests itself in myriad ways: motives, thoughts, words, and actions. Many people hear the word "sin" and immediately think of "bad things," things we're not supposed to do: lying, cheating, beating little brother with a stick. But sin is not simply doing bad things; it's putting good things in the place of God. All sin boils down to the worship or cherishing of created things rather than the Creator.[6] Anytime we prize and pursue something more than we prize God himself, even if this thing is not inherently evil, we have committed a sin. My children display their sinful hearts all the time, but especially during the month of December. Their Christmas lists, conversations, and actions all reveal that their first love is not God, but Nerf guns. Not even Jerry Falwell would put Nerf guns on his list of forbidden pleasures. They don't fit the category of "bad things." But when they become my boys' greatest desire, God is displeased. Both sin and salvation can be summarized in one word: *substitution.* Sin is finding some substitute for God, worshiping something else in his place. Salvation comes when God sends a substitute for us, punishing someone else in our place. We'll come back to the idea of substitution in the next chapter.

In sum, our natural state is not one of intimacy with God, but of hostility, which brings judgment. The reason for this is our sinful nature inherited from our first parents, which manifests itself in sinful behavior, the worship of created things rather than our Creator. The bad news, then, is *really* bad. The God of the universe is *against us.* This is why Jesus came to earth: to do something about this dreadful preposition—*against.* In fact, as we will see, Jesus is Immanuel, God *with* us. And he came so that God could once again be *for* us. Good theology is all about the prepositions, really.

THE SON WITH NO BEGINNING: JESUS' DEITY

The second line of the Creed begins, "I believe in Jesus Christ, his only Son, our Lord." Christian faith cannot be reduced to the assertion that a real character named Jesus once walked the earth. The question each person must answer is the one asked in Matthew 16:15: *Who is Jesus?* The name "Jesus" literally means "God saves." At the beginning of Matthew's Gospel, an angel appears to Joseph and declares, "[Mary] will bear a son, and you are to name him Jesus, for he will save his people from their sins."[7] There is a widespread notion that Jesus and Christ are both names, but this is incorrect. Jesus doesn't walk into the room 007 style, order his martini shaken, not stirred, and say, "The name's *Christ, Jesus Christ.*" Christ is not a surname, except perhaps in the old sense in which surnames declared a person's profession: Samuel *Smith* or Thomas *Taylor*.[8] Strictly speaking, we ought to say "Jesus, *the* Christ." Jesus is a name, and Christ is a title.

The title "Christ" is a translation of the Greek term

Christos, which itself is a translation of the Hebrew term *Maschiach*. The basic sense of *Maschiach* is "anointed one." In the Old Testament, people were anointed as a way of being set apart for some special service. In Israel, priests were anointed, as were kings. King David is often referred to as "the anointed of God." But David was not the greatest king. The covenant or holy promise God made to David was that one of his descendants would rule forever. In 2 Samuel 7:12–14, the word of the Lord comes to David: "When your days are fulfilled and you lie down with your ancestors, I will raise up your offspring after you, who shall come forth from your body, and I will establish his kingdom. He shall build a house for my name, and I will establish the throne of his kingdom forever. I will be a father to him, and he shall be a son to me." In calling Jesus the Christ, the New Testament writers declare that he is the long-awaited Savior-King, the one promised within the pages of the Old Testament.

Jesus, the anointed one of God, is also God's "only Son," meaning that he is the unique Son, the only one of his class.[9] When applied to Jesus, the title "Son of God" is a clear affirmation of his deity. We use the popular expression "Like father, like son" to point out that a human child shares the nature of his father. In the same way, Jesus the Son shares the nature of God the Father; he is of equal status or "Godness" with the Father.[10] The author of Hebrews writes, "Long ago God spoke to our ancestors in many and various ways by the prophets, but in these last days he has spoken to us by a Son, whom he appointed heir of all things, through whom he also created the worlds. [This Son] is the reflection of God's glory and the exact imprint of God's very being, and he sustains all things by his powerful word."[11] Note that the Son is the "exact imprint of God's very being" and that it was "through the Son" that God the Father created all things. John plays the same tune in his Gospel: "In the beginning was the Word [i.e., Jesus], and the Word was with God, and the Word was God. He was in the beginning with God. All things came into being through him, and without him not one thing came into being."[12] When John uses the phrase "In the beginning," he means "Before the beginning of the world." Both John and the writer of Hebrews are emphasizing the *eternality* of the Son and his *equality* with the Father. Though Jesus was *born* in Bethlehem (as we will discuss momentarily), he did not *begin* in Bethlehem. He is the Son with no beginning.

The final designation we find in this line of the Creed is "Lord." In the Old Testament, this title is given repeatedly to

God. In Genesis we read, "Then the LORD God formed man from the dust of the ground, and breathed into his nostrils the breath of life; and the man became a living being."[13] The Psalmist cries out, "My mouth will tell of your righteous acts, of your deeds of salvation all day long, though their number is past my knowledge. I will come praising the mighty deeds of the LORD GOD, I will praise your righteousness, yours alone."[14] The most fundamental confession of the Old Testament is: "The LORD our God, the LORD is one."[15] When we come to the New Testament, a stunning development has taken place, which is captured in 1 Corinthians 8:6: "For us there is one God, the Father, from whom are all things and for whom we exist, *and one Lord, Jesus Christ*, through whom are all things and through whom we exist."[16] In their writings and worship practices, the earliest Christians recognized that Jesus had the same right to lordship as God himself.[17]

What was it that caused the early believers to speak of Jesus as Lord? What was listed on his résumé? Resurrection from the dead! In Romans 10:9, Paul explains, "If you confess with your lips that Jesus is Lord and believe in your heart that God raised him from the dead, you will be saved." Jesus' teaching and the many miracles he performed during his earthly ministry pointed to the truth that he was no ordinary man, but his defeat of death was the supreme demonstration of his deity.[18] As Paul says, he was "declared with power to be the Son of God by his resurrection from the dead."[19] In the next chapter, we'll talk more about the resurrection. For now, notice that, according to the Creed, Jesus is not just the Lord, but he is "our Lord." Believers are Christ's property; he has acquired us for himself through his blood.[20] To recognize Jesus as Lord is to submit to him, to seek to do his will. And the lordship of Jesus, properly understood, limits every other allegiance. When we confess that Jesus Christ, God's Son, is our Lord, we are saying that our ultimate commitment is not to our nation, not to our employers, not to our family or friends, but to him.[21]

GOD WITH MEAT: JESUS' HUMANITY

Thus far we have explored some of the biblical passages that emphasize the deity of Jesus: he is *the eternal Son of God*. We need now to think about the journey Jesus took to this earth. Theologians refer to this as the *incarnation*. Every fall I find myself craving chili. If I go to the store to pick up a can of *chile con carne*, it means I'm in the mood for meat. *Chile con carne* is "chili with meat." The word "incarnation" means "God with meat." The term refers to *the enfleshment of the eternal Son of God*. Karl Barth calls the incarnation "the divine condescension."[22] Remaining what he was—fully God—Jesus became what he was not—fully man. The greatness of God came down to us in the smallness of the child in the manger. The Son with no beginning was born in Bethlehem. As the Creed says: "He was conceived by the power of the Holy Spirit and born of the Virgin Mary."

This section of the Creed expresses key elements of the angelic encounters recorded in Matthew 1:18–25 and Luke 1:26–38. It will be worthwhile to read the Luke account in full:

> *In the sixth month the angel Gabriel was sent by God to a town in Galilee called Nazareth, to a virgin engaged to a man whose name was Joseph, of the house of David. The virgin's name was Mary. And he came to her and said, 'Greetings, favored one! The Lord is with you.' But she was much perplexed by his words and pondered what sort of greeting this might be. The angel said to her, 'Do not be afraid, Mary, for you have found favor with God. And now, you will conceive in your womb and bear a son, and you will name him Jesus. He will be great, and will be called the Son of the*

Most High, and the Lord God will give to him the throne of his ancestor David. He will reign over the house of Jacob forever, and of his kingdom there will be no end.' Mary said to the angel, 'How can this be, since I am a virgin?' The angel said to her, 'The Holy Spirit will come upon you, and the power of the Most High will overshadow you; therefore the child to be born will be holy; he will be called Son of God. And now, your relative Elizabeth in her old age has also conceived a son; and this is the sixth month for her who was said to be barren. For nothing will be impossible with God.' Then Mary said, 'Here am I, the servant of the Lord; let it be with me according to your word.' Then the angel departed from her.

I imagine it was a typical Tuesday in Nazareth. In today's terms, Mary had just finished her 5:30 a.m. WOD at Cross-Fit. On her way home, she stopped by Starbucks to pick up a Skinny Peppermint Mocha. She had to watch her figure, of course, because she was "engaged" or "betrothed." Betrothal was the first of a two-step Jewish marriage process. It involved a formal witnessed agreement to marry and an exchange of a bride price. At this point, the woman and the man were legally bound, though the marriage would not be consummated until roughly a year later. As strange as it seems to us today, in the ancient world a girl could be betrothed to a man as early as age twelve. Most biblical scholars believe that Mary was between twelve and fifteen at this time. So picture teenage Mary, whose day is off to a remarkably ordinary start, when suddenly a messenger from God appears.[23] And at Starbucks of all places. They're the ones who take the Christ out of Christmas with their plain red cups! (The lot of complaining Christians need to find better things to do.)

The angel's message for Mary is more than bloggable. "Mary," he says, "you are going to be pregnant...*with God*." She must have spilled the Peppermint Mocha all over herself. Mary eventually believes this message and surrenders herself to God's plan. But her initial reaction is one of inquiry: "How can this be, since I am a virgin?" The angel explains that the Holy Spirit will bring life to Mary's womb. How pregnancy can result from contact with the Holy Spirit is a question the Creed (and the Bible) leaves unanswered. We should not think of the Holy Spirit as the father of Jesus. As Karl Barth quips, "There was no wedding between the Holy Spirit and Mary!"[24] All we can say is that God the Father planned the birth of

Jesus, and that it occurred by the intervention of the Holy Spirit in Mary's womb. Inside Mary's body, Jesus became a human being in precisely the same way we all are, yet without sin.[25] Jesus did not simply *appear* to be human; he actually *became* human. The witness of Scripture is that Jesus was born through all the embryonic processes of the womb. He had real blood running through his veins. He grew in wisdom and stature, experienced hunger and thirst, felt grief and pain, fought temptation.[26] And yet while the flesh of Jesus is the same as our flesh, he was born not as other men are born, not of the will of an earthly father. As the prophet Isaiah predicted some seven hundred years before it took place, this was a virginal conception.[27]

These are big words—"virginal conception"—that require quite a bit of unpacking. My five- and seven-year-old boys aren't ready for basic biology discussions yet, but this doesn't mean that I need to wait until later to teach them about Jesus' birth. When we talk about Jesus' journey to earth, I generally say something like, "Jesus was born in a special way to show us that he is both human and God." We'll talk about the "natural way" of conception as my boys get older, and then they'll understand exactly how Jesus' birth was "special" or "supernatural." The virginal conception is indeed an important tenet of

Christianity, so in due time we need to teach our children about it.[28] The miracle of Jesus' conception reminds us that we cannot produce our own Savior; salvation is a gift that comes from outside us, "not from humanity's own inherent possibilities."[29]

THE MISSION OF THE GOD-MAN

Scripture doesn't tell us when or how it happened, but sometime after the angel appeared to Mary, Mary informed Joseph that she was pregnant. In Matthew 1:18–25, we learn that, at first, Joseph didn't believe Mary's story about an angel and a pregnancy resulting from the power of the Holy Spirit. Joseph probably didn't know Mary very well at this stage. Back then, betrothed couples had very little interaction with each other. Joseph didn't know Mary's favorite flower, her favorite movie, or what she had on her 5k playlist. Being relatively unacquainted with his betrothed, Joseph had no reason to believe her crazy story. All he heard Mary say was, "I'm pregnant." Joseph knew that he had not been with Mary. So the only logical conclusion was that his bride-to-be had been unfaithful. Joseph was devastated, heartbroken, and it was at this very moment that God sent an angel to corroborate Mary's story, to heal Joseph's pain.

This is the magnificent thing about the God of the Bible: he cares about all the hurting in the world. He is not a detached deity, a God so overwhelmed by his cosmic chore list that he has no time for his crying children. In the first Chronicles of Narnia book, *The Magician's Nephew*, the young boy Digory meets Aslan, the Great Lion, in the newly created land of Narnia. Digory's mother, back home in London, is very sick. In fact, she's dying. Concerned for his mother, and cognizant of the Lion's power, Digory makes a request of Aslan: "Please, please—won't you—can't you give me something that will cure Mother?" We read on:

> *Up till then [Digory] had been looking at the Lion's great feet and the huge claws on them; now, in his despair, he looked up at its face. What he saw surprised him as much as anything in his whole life. For the tawny face was bent down near his own and (wonder of wonders) great shining tears stood in the Lion's eyes. They were such big, bright tears compared with Digory's own that for a moment he felt as if the Lion must really be sorrier about his Mother than he was himself.*[30]

The Christian God cares about our pain. He cared enough to enter into our pain-stricken, sin-sick world in order to bring healing. Jesus Christ came to restore the relationship of intimacy that once existed between God and humanity. He is the "one mediator between God and men," precisely because he is both God and man.[31] In other words, his *identity* indicates his *mission*.[32] Jesus, the God-Man, came to bring God to man and man to God. In the next chapter, we will look at exactly *how* Jesus reconciles us to God.

FAMILY WORSHIP GUIDE

The Apostles' Creed

As a family, memorize the second part of the Creed in three simple steps:

> *I believe in Jesus Christ, his only Son, our Lord.*
> *He was conceived by the power of the Holy Spirit*
> *and born of the Virgin Mary.*

Key Verses

In addition to memorizing the second part of the Creed, choose one or more of the following passages to treasure in your heart:

WE ARE SINNERS

> *For all have sinned and fall short of the glory of God. (Romans 3:23 NIV)*
> *For the wages of sin is death, but the gift of God is eternal life in Christ Jesus our Lord. (Romans 6:23 NIV)*

JESUS IS FULLY GOD

> *In the beginning was the Word [Jesus], and the Word was with God, and the Word was God. He was with God in the*

beginning. Through him all things were made; without him
nothing was made that has been made. (John 1:1–3 NIV)

REMAINING FULLY GOD, JESUS BECAME FULLY MAN

She will give birth to a son, and you are to give him the
name Jesus, because he will save his people from their sins.
(Matthew 1:21 NIV)

THE GOD-MAN IS THE MEDIATOR

For there is one God and one mediator between God and
mankind, the man Christ Jesus. (1 Timothy 2:5 NIV)

Nuggets of Truth

Parent-theologians, when teaching your children-disciples, be sure
to cover these main points from Chapter 2:

OF APPLE TREES AND APPLES: HUMANITY'S SINFULNESS

- The name "Adam" means "man" or "mankind." As the first
  man, Adam served as a representative. God placed him in
  the Garden to act not simply for himself, but also for all of
  his future descendants.

- The doctrine of *original sin* means that, as descendants of
  Adam, we are sinful or corrupt to the very core of our being.

- Our sinful nature shows itself in many ways: motives, thoughts, words, and actions.

- Sin is not simply doing bad things; it's putting good things in the place of God. All sin boils down to the worship or cherishing of created things rather than the Creator.

- As sinners, our relationship with God is not one of intimacy or friendship, but of hostility or war. We deserve God's judgment (eternal punishment).

THE SON WITH NO BEGINNING: JESUS' DEITY

- The name "Jesus" means "God saves."

- In calling Jesus "the Christ," the New Testament writers declare that he is the long-awaited Savior-King, the one promised within the pages of the Old Testament.

- When applied to Jesus, the title "Son of God" is a way of saying that he shares the nature of God the Father; he is of equal status or "Godness" with the Father.

- Jesus has the same right to lordship as God the Father. His teaching and the many miracles he performed during his earthly ministry pointed to the truth that he was no ordinary man, but his defeat of death was the supreme demonstration of his lordship.

GOD WITH MEAT: JESUS' HUMANITY

- The term "incarnation" means "God with meat." It refers to the enfleshment of the eternal Son of God. Remaining what he was—fully God—Jesus became what he was not—fully man.

- God the Father planned the birth of Jesus, and it occurred by the intervention of the Holy Spirit. Inside Mary's body, Jesus became a human being in precisely the same way we all are, yet without sin.

- Without getting into human biology, we can explain the miracle of Jesus' birth to our children by saying something like, "Jesus was born in a special way to show us that he is both human and God."

- As our children get older, we can fill in the details, explaining that the virginal conception reminds us that we cannot produce our own Savior; salvation is a gift that comes from outside us, not from our own inherent possibilities.

THE MISSION OF THE GOD-MAN

- Jesus Christ came to restore the relationship of intimacy that once existed between God and humanity. Jesus, the God-Man, came to bring God to man and man to God.

Questions for the Family

Use these questions to spark discussion during your family worship times:

OF APPLE TREES AND APPLES: HUMANITY'S SINFULNESS

- What does the name "Adam" mean, and why is this important?

- What is sin?

- What are some examples of sin from our own lives?

- What does sin do to our relationship with God?

THE SON WITH NO BEGINNING: JESUS' DEITY

- What does the Bible mean when it calls Jesus the "Son of God"?

- What does it mean to confess that Jesus is "our Lord"?

GOD WITH MEAT: JESUS' HUMANITY

- What does the word "incarnation" mean?

- How is Jesus like us? How is he unlike us?

- What does the identity of Jesus (the God-Man) tell us about what he came to earth to do?

Songs That Celebrate These Truths

As you study the truths summarized in part two of the Creed, also celebrate these truths as a family. Sing the following songs together, and try to memorize at least the first verse of each one.

- "Once in Royal David's City"

- "Go, Tell It on the Mountain"

Prayer Prompts

Always conclude your family worship times with prayer. Here are some prayer themes to keep in mind while your family studies this part of the Creed:

- Our sinful hearts, and thus our need for salvation

- An awareness of our sinful behavior

- The truth of Jesus, God's Son, leaving his place in heaven and coming to earth for us

- The lordship of Jesus in our own lives

3
The Son's Death and Resurrection

He suffered under Pontius Pilate, was crucified,
died, and was buried. He descended to the dead.
On the third day he rose again.

THE CHALLENGE OF EXPLAINING THE CROSS TO OUR CHILDREN

As my boys, Aidan and Cullen, were memorizing the Apostles' Creed, I had to correct them on a number of points. For a while, Cullen consistently replaced "the Holy Spirit" with "the whole experience." A charismatic in the making. But the most humorous error occurred as the boys were learning the portion of the Creed that will be our focus in this chapter. Countless times I had to remind them, "No, boys, it's Pontius *Pilate*, not Pontius *Privates*." For children, this is indeed a difficult section of the Creed, and not just because it mentions a government official who can easily be mistaken for genitalia. How do we explain the gory punishment of crucifixion to young children? And most important, how do we articulate the saving work of Christ in such a way that our children understand God's love for them? In other words, how do we help them see, not just the *event* of the cross, but also the *meaning* of the cross?

The Australian scholar Leon Morris is right to describe the cross as a multifaceted gem.[1] With each turn of the gem, we gain a more complete understanding of our salvation. For example, the New Testament speaks of salvation as *redemption*. "In [Christ] we have redemption through his blood, the forgiveness of our trespasses, according to the riches of his grace."[2] As we study this facet, we come to appreciate that a great ransom has been paid to set us free from sin.[3] Additionally, Scripture refers to salvation as *justification*. "Much more surely then, now that we have been justified by his blood, will we be saved through him from the wrath of God."[4] Examining this word-picture, we discover that we stand guilty before God in his courtroom, and it is only through faith in Christ, the one who fulfilled God's righteous requirements for us, that we are exonerated.

Still another way the New Testament describes salvation is as *reconciliation*. This is the facet I have opted to focus on in this chapter, because in my experience it is the easiest for a child to comprehend. Reconciliation has to do with conflict being resolved. Or to state the matter in more child-friendly terms, *it is about enemies becoming friends.* As we have learned, since the time of Genesis 3, a terrible conflict has existed between God and humanity. Jesus is the only one who can put an end to this conflict. We saw in the previous chapter that Christ came to earth as "the embodied communion between God and man."[5] His identity indicates his mission: the God-man came to bring God to man and man to God. It is Jesus' whole life, and above all his life poured out in the supreme sacrifice on the cross, that brings the hostility between the holy God and sinful humanity to an end.

THE EVENT OF THE CRUCIFIXION: WHAT HAPPENED AT GOLGOTHA?

The Creed continues, "He suffered under Pontius Pilate, was crucified, died, and was buried." Pontius Pilate was an aristocrat appointed by the Roman Emperor Tiberius. He served as the prefect of the Roman province of Judea from AD 26 to 36. In regards to his character, Pilate was "a thug in a toga."[6] The first-century Jewish authors Philo and Josephus have nothing but contempt for ole Pontius Privates (they would prefer this name). It's interesting, then, that Pilate is the only other person, besides Jesus and Mary, named in the ancient Christian creeds. We find no mention of Abraham or Paul, Moses or Peter. Why the reference to this Roman ruffian? The inclusion of Pilate is important; it anchors the suffering of Jesus in history. When we discuss the crucifixion, we are dealing not with some fairy tale, but with an actual occurrence, a datable event.

All four Gospel writers describe this event. The crucifixion of Christ took place at Golgotha, "Place of a Skull."[7] We don't know how Golgotha acquired its name. Maybe it was because this was a popular site for Roman executions. Perhaps it was because there were numerous tombs nearby. Certainly it was a place that reeked of death. Jesus began his journey to the Skull carrying his cross, a beam that would have weighed at least thirty or forty pounds. The walk was long for a man who had endured a scourging, an excruciating punishment involving a leather whip with pieces of lead or bone attached to its ends. Weak from the loss of blood, Jesus collapsed, so the soldiers grabbed a man from the crowd and forced him to carry the cross the remainder of the way. This man's name was Simon of Cyrene. In Mark's Gospel, we learn that Simon was a father.

He had two boys, Alexander and Rufus.[8] As parent-theologians explain the crucifixion to their children, they should pause and contemplate this point: "I wonder if Alexander and Rufus were present that day, the day their father carried the cross for Jesus. Did they see Jesus collapse under the weight of his cross? Did they see him suffering?" This will prove helpful later as parents make the point that, whether or not Simon's boys were physically present that day, *we were present* in the sense that Jesus was being punished for our sins.

When they arrived at Golgotha, a number of things could have happened; it's difficult to be precise. The Romans employed a number of different crucifixion techniques, each of them horrific. The word "crucifixion" would have sent a shudder down the spine of any educated person in the ancient world.[9] It was a savagely cruel way of eliminating undesirables, a form of execution that brought agony and the maximum amount of degradation and humiliation before death. Classical Roman authors are reluctant to write of crucifixion in any detail, presumably because of its gruesome nature. The Roman writer Seneca offers a brief report on his experience with crucifixion. He claims to have witnessed many different types of crosses: some that stretch the victim's arms out on the crossbeam, some that hang the victim upside down, and some that impale the victim's reproductive organs.[10] Once tied or nailed to the cross, the victim found it very difficult to breathe, due to the strain placed on the chest by the weight of the body. To prolong the suffering, Roman executioners would sometimes place a small wooden seat on the upright beam of the cross, allowing the victim to struggle for air a little longer. Eventually, the person would die from exhaustion, unable to breathe.

This is what happened to Jesus. After enduring the torment for many hours, Christ called out with a loud voice, "Father, into your hands I commend my spirit!"[11] When he said this, he took his last breath. Jesus was dead. Surely he was dead. Jesus didn't just faint from injury. He suffered at the hands of experienced Roman executioners. The cross on which Jesus hung was far from unique. Crucifixion was the common way in which the Romans punished criminals. On occasion, thousands of people were crucified at the same time, with their bodies lining the highways.[12] Is it really likely that expert Roman executioners would have botched Jesus' execution?[13] The Son of God died, and his body was placed in a tomb. But the tomb was impotent; death could not hold him.

Crucifixion is the sort of thing that can give even a grown man nightmares. While adults need to understand the magnitude of suffering Jesus endured for his people, they will need to use discretion as they describe crucifixion to the children under their care. Depending on the age of the child, certain details may need to be omitted. Such omission does not mean that a parent has diluted the gospel. There is a difference between understanding the *mechanics* of Christ's crucifixion and affirming the *meaning* of this event. Particulars of Roman crucifixion, such as the use of nails to hang the victim on the cross, may or may not be shared. The pivotal point to emphasize at this stage is that *Christ actually suffered and died.* Once this has been made clear, we must turn to the crucial question: "Why?" Christianity is not merely about the historical fact that Jesus Christ died on a cross; essentially, it is about the wonderful truth that *Christ died so that we can be forgiven.*

THE DILEMMA OF OUR PARDON: WHY CAN'T GOD JUST FORGIVE US?

Every time I enter a Barnes & Noble, I'm amazed, because it seems that since my last visit, the self-help section has doubled in size. Like the Blob from the old sci-fi film, this section of the bookstore just grows and grows. People today want to improve themselves and their position in life, and the self-help section has all the answers. Interestingly, it seems that most of life's problems can be solved with kale. As comedian Jim Gaffigan says, kale is a superfood; its special power is tasting like bug spray. Against the world's best-selling genre, Christianity contends that our natural state is one of *self-helplessness*. Remember the terrible conflict that exists between God and humanity, the conflict that goes all the way back to the Garden of Eden. We are unable to repair our relationship with God, not only because we are enslaved to sin and therefore do not desire intimacy with God, but also because we have sinned *against God* and therefore *only God* can forgive and restore us. Even if we did desire reconciliation with God, this alone would not be enough to secure our forgiveness. Since our sin is against God, God must act to forgive.

But God cannot simply forgive sinners. The reason for this is his character. According to 2 Timothy 2:13, the one thing God cannot do is "deny himself." To quote Michael Bird, "The only limit to [God's] power is the contours of his character and the consistency of his nature."[14] This means that God must respond to the reality of human rebellion in a way that is congruous with his character, as it has been revealed to us in the Scriptures. The witness of Scripture is that God is loving and merciful, but the Bible is equally clear that God is holy and just. God's holiness has to do with his purity and moral perfection. Because God is holy, he despises sin; our sin provokes his wrath. This is not the wicked, resentful, and malicious anger we find among humans.[15] It is the right reaction of the perfectly pure God toward his now sinful creatures. With this holy hostility comes judgment. God is not just—he does not behave in a way that is *right*—unless he inflicts upon all sin and evil the punishment it deserves. The appropriate punishment for sin is death, physical as well as spiritual, loss of the body as well as eternal separation from the loving and life-giving presence of God.[16] This is the rightful sentence that God has announced against us and now must inflict. Herein lies the dilemma of our forgiveness. Confronted by human evil, how could God be true to himself as both loving and holy? He could not both pardon and punish us. Hence, the necessity of *substitution. God remained true to himself by punishing his appointed substitute so that his love could be directed toward us in forgiveness.*[17]

This idea of substitution is introduced in the Old Testament sacrificial system. For many people, the sacrifices outlined in Leviticus are confusing and probably even frightening. This is because the concept of sacrifice is totally foreign to our world.

When was the last time you walked over to the neighbor's place to borrow his pressure washer and had to wait until he finished sacrificing some livestock? (If this has happened to you recently, it might be time to find a new neighborhood. Just a suggestion.) The sacrificial system of the Old Testament was elaborate. It called for daily, weekly, monthly, and occasional offerings. The five main types of offerings are prescribed in the early chapters of Leviticus. The blood sacrifices all shared the same basic ritual. It began with the worshipper bringing the animal, laying his hands on the head of the animal, and then killing it. As John Stott puts it, "This was significant symbolism, not meaningless magic."[18] It was a *symbolic* transferal of the sins of the worshipper to the animal, and the animal was then killed *instead of* the worshipper.

It's unfortunate that many children's Bibles spend little or no time on the Old Testament sacrificial system, because the animal sacrifices can serve as potent object lessons for children. In my home study I have a sheepskin that I received years ago when I pastored a church on the south island of New Zealand, a place where there are more sheep than people. I've often asked my boys to place their hands on this sheepskin and imagine the times when God told his people to place their hands on the animals they slew. I usually say something like this: "God's people put their hands on the head of the animal and then killed it because they were sinners, and the Bible teaches us that for a sinner to be forgiven by the holy God, something must die in the sinner's place." We must then go on to explain that, though the Old Testament sacrifices pointed out *the way of salvation*, the sacrifices themselves *had no saving power*. The writer of Hebrews tells us, "Without the shedding of blood there is no forgiveness of sins."[19] But this same writer insists, "It is impossible for the blood of bulls and goats to take away sins."[20] The blood of animals could never cope with the problems of man. But these sacrifices stated emphatically, "For sinful people to be pardoned, something must perish in their place."

THE PERFECT SUBSTITUTE: WHAT IS THE *MEANING* OF THE CROSS AND THE EMPTY TOMB?

The death of Jesus is the sacrifice that *accomplished* what the Old Testament sacrifices pointed to but could not do.[21] Jesus is the *perfect substitute*, who died so that we can be forgiven. Here we must return to the pivotal idea, introduced in the previous chapter, that *the person of Christ and the work of Christ cannot be separated.* Being God and man in one person, Jesus acts from the side of God *as God* and from the side of man *as man.*[22] God is the one who created us. God is the one against whom we have sinned. God therefore must be the one who acts to forgive our sin. He does so in Jesus, who also is man and thus is able to be our substitute. Jesus lived a life of perfect obedience, fulfilling God's righteous requirements for us, and he died the death of a sinner, absorbing God's holy hostility for us.

When Paul and other New Testament writers refer to Jesus as the *propitiation* for our sins, they mean that he is the Wrath-Quencher, the Anger-Eraser.[23] Jesus is the answer to the riddle of Exodus 34:6–7: "The LORD, the LORD, a God merciful and gracious, slow to anger, and abounding in steadfast love and faithfulness, keeping steadfast love for the thousandth generation, forgiving iniquity and transgression and sin, *yet by no means clearing the guilty.*" Jesus is the answer to the questions: How can God be true to himself as both loving and holy? How can he both pardon and punish sin? Jesus is the one who both extinguishes the wrath of God and exhibits the love of God. J. I. Packer puts it beautifully: "Jesus Christ our Lord, moved by a love that was determined to do everything necessary to save us, endured and exhausted the destructive divine judgment for which we were otherwise inescapably destined."[24]

In Sid Fleischman's Newbery Medal–winning book, *The Whipping Boy*, we embark on an adventure with a spoiled prince, Prince Brat, and the orphaned whipping boy, Jemmy. At the beginning of the story, the prince is quite the hellion, but as Fleischman puts it: "Prince Brat knew that he had nothing to fear. He had never been spanked in his life. He was a prince! And it was forbidden to spank, thrash, cuff, smack, or whip a prince. A common boy was kept in the castle to be punished in his place."[25] The whipping boy is analogous to Christ. But of course, Christ wasn't "plucked from the streets and sewers of the city to serve as royal whipping boy."[26] Because of his profound love for us, Christ willingly surrendered his place in heaven and came to earth to deal with the dilemma of our sin. As the Apostle Paul says, the Son of God "emptied himself, taking the form of a slave, being born in human likeness. And being found in human form, he humbled himself and became obedient to the point of death—even death on a cross."[27]

The denomination in which I grew up sometimes is guilty of leaving Jesus on the cross. This is not to suggest that they denied the bodily resurrection of Christ—by no means—but it is to say that they got so hyped up about Christ's sacrifice on Good Friday that they commonly ran out of steam before getting to Holy Saturday and Resurrection Sunday.[28] This is a bit like quitting at mile thirteen in a marathon. The Apostles' Creed causes us to press on: "He suffered under Pontius Pilate, was crucified, died, and was buried. *He descended to the dead. On the third day he rose again.*" "He descended to the dead" is the most controversial clause of the Creed. For some biblical scholars, this line means simply that Jesus actually died. Others interpret the clause as a reference to Jesus' descent to hell, but this is unlikely because it seems that hell either does not exist or is not populated until the time of Revelation 20:14. I tend to side with those who read this line of the Creed as a reference to Jesus' descent to the waiting place of the dead, which Scripture frequently refers to as Hades or Sheol. Consider the question: What did Jesus do on Saturday, the period between his death and bodily resurrection? My suggestion is that, while his body was in the tomb, the immaterial part of his person descended to the underworld, where he both proclaimed his victory over the forces of evil and set free the saints of old, God's people who passed from this world prior to the cross.[29] Since Holy Saturday, believers who die go directly to heaven to be with Christ, though heaven is *not* the ultimate hope of the Christ-follower, as we will see in the next chapter.

Jesus Christ, the sufferer of Good Friday and the proclaimer of Holy Saturday, is also the victor of Easter Sunday. Children (and maybe adults) are easily confused by the claim that Jesus was raised on the *third* day. In the ancient world, any part of a day constituted a whole day; thus, late Friday afternoon to early Sunday morning equaled three days. In 1 Corinthians 15, Paul says that when Jesus was raised on the third day, he appeared to more than five hundred people. There was no shortage of eyewitnesses! The Gospels tell us about specific people who encountered the risen Christ, and these accounts make it clear that Jesus exited the tomb in *physical form*. In John 20, we read of Thomas touching Jesus' wounds. The Son of God did not seep out of the tomb as a spirit or ghost. Jesus had a body. He had a shoe size. I imagine he preferred size 12 Nike Metcons.

We'll talk more about the resurrection of the body as we make our way through the Apostles' Creed. In the final part of this section, we need to shift from the *occasion* of the resurrection to the *significance* of the occasion. What does the resurrection *mean*?

The resurrection is the revelation of the Father's *acceptance* of the life and death of Jesus as full and sufficient sacrifice. As Thomas Torrance says, it is "God's great act of *amen* to the cross."[30] In Mark 2:1–12, Jesus is preaching, and a paralytic is brought to him, lowered down through the roof. Jesus says to the man, "Son, your sins are forgiven." When the scribes hear this pronouncement, they question Jesus: "Who can forgive sins but God alone?" Jesus proceeds to say, "Which is easier, to say to the paralytic, 'Your sins are forgiven,' or to say, 'Stand up and take up your mat and walk'? *But so that you may know* that the Son of Man has authority on earth to forgive sins I say to you, *stand up, take your mat and go to your home.*" The empty tomb is the "so that you may know"—the verification of forgiveness. Without the resurrection of Christ, there would be no reason to think that the crucifixion actually dealt with our sin. But with the resurrection, we are assured that our fellowship with God is restored.

With the resurrection of Jesus, we are also assured that death will not be the end for us. Christ endured death for us, and he *defeated* death for us. Think of death as an enormous beast who attacks Jesus, but the beast is put down. If your children are old enough to watch the *Lord of the Rings* movies, remind them of the wonderful scene that spans the first two films where Gandalf, having been dragged into the abyss by the Balrog, battles the ancient demon on the descent and then emerges victorious. Just as J.R.R. Tolkien's wizard defeats this horror that threatened the life of every member of the fellowship, so the Son of God conquered the monster of death for us. Jesus Christ has been raised from the dead, and according to 1 Corinthians 15:20, he is the "firstfruits" of a much greater harvest. What this means is that the resurrection of Christ is not an *isolated incident*; all those who believe in Christ will one day be raised just as Christ himself was raised. We are the harvest!

"LOOK TO JESUS"

Let's wrap things up with a child-friendly summary statement and a brief but powerful story. The doctrines expounded in this chapter can be stated simply: *Jesus died on the cross for our sins and was raised on the third day, and when we believe this, we are forgiven of our sins and become forever friends with God.* The nineteenth-century Baptist preacher Charles Spurgeon wrote in his autobiography that this strange doctrine of the substitutionary death of Christ is one of the surest proofs of the divine inspiration of Scripture. "Who would or could have thought of the just Ruler dying for the unjust rebel?" God himself must have ordained it; it is not a matter that any man could have imagined.

The story of how Spurgeon became a Christian is one of the best-known conversion stories in the history of the church.[31] It was a wintry Sunday in January 1850. Spurgeon's school had been closed due to an outbreak of fever. He was wandering around Colchester when the snow and sleet suddenly started getting worse, so he went looking for cover. Turning down a side lane called Artillery Street, he came to a little Primitive Methodist Chapel. The morning service was just beginning. There were no more than fifteen people present. The minister had failed to arrive because of the weather, so into the pulpit climbed a thin-faced man, not a preacher, but a shoemaker or tailor. Spurgeon was never to know anything about him. The man announced his text: Isaiah 45:22, "Look unto me, and be ye saved, all the ends of the earth." Spurgeon writes, "He was obliged to stick to the text, for the simple reason that he had little else to say." The man began, "My dear friends, this is a very simple text indeed. It says, 'Look.' Now lookin' don't take a deal of pain. It ain't liftin' your foot or your finger; it is just 'Look!' Well, a man needn't go to college to learn to look. You may be the biggest fool, and yet you can look. A man needn't be worth a thousand a year to be able to look. Anyone can look; even a child can look."

After a while, the preacher turned to Spurgeon and said,

"Young man, you look very miserable." "Well," writes Spurgeon, "I did look miserable, but I had not been accustomed to have remarks made from the pulpit on my personal appearance before. However, it was a good blow, struck right home." The preacher went on, "And you always will be miserable—miserable in life and miserable in death—if you don't obey my text; but if you obey now, this moment, you will be saved." Then the man shouted at the top of his voice, "Young man, look to Jesus Christ. Look! Look! Look! You have nothing to do but to look and live!" Spurgeon writes in his autobiography, "I saw at once the way of salvation. I know not what else he said—I did not take much notice of it—I was so possessed with that one thought.... Oh! I looked until I could almost have looked my eyes away. There and then the cloud was gone, the darkness had rolled away, and that moment I saw the sun; and I could have risen that instant, and sung with the most enthusiastic of them, of the precious blood of Christ, and the simple faith which looks alone to Him."

The shoemaker got it right: "Even a child can look to Jesus." And the responsibility of parent-theologians is to direct and help focus their children's eyes. In short, the task is a telescopic one: help your children see the person and work of Jesus more clearly.

FAMILY WORSHIP GUIDE

The Apostles' Creed

As a family, memorize the third part of the Creed in three simple steps:

> *He suffered under Pontius Pilate, was crucified, died,*
> > *and was buried.*
> *He descended to the dead.*
> *On the third day he rose again.*

Key Verses

In addition to memorizing the third part of the Creed, choose one or more of the following passages to treasure in your heart:

GOD AS LOVING AND HOLY

> *The LORD, the LORD, the compassionate and gracious God, slow to anger, abounding in love and faithfulness, maintaining love to thousands, and forgiving wickedness, rebellion and sin. Yet he does not leave the guilty unpunished. (Exodus 34:6–7 NIV)*

CHRIST AS OUR SUBSTITUTE

But God demonstrates his own love for us in this: While we were still sinners, Christ died for us. (Romans 5:8 NIV)

For what I received I passed on to you as of first importance: that Christ died for our sins according to the Scriptures, that he was buried, that he was raised on the third day according to the Scriptures. (1 Corinthians 15:3–4 NIV)

In this the love of God was made manifest among us, that God sent his only Son into the world, so that we might live through him. In this is love, not that we have loved God but that he loved us and sent his Son to be the propitiation for our sins. (1 John 4:9–10 ESV)

CHRIST AS THE FIRSTFRUITS

But Christ has indeed been raised from the dead, the first-fruits of those who have fallen asleep. For since death came through a man, the resurrection of the dead comes also through a man. For as in Adam all die, so in Christ all will be made alive. (1 Corinthians 15:20–22 NIV)

Nuggets of Truth

Parent-theologians, when teaching your children-disciples, be sure to cover these main points from Chapter 3:

THE EVENT OF THE CRUCIFIXION: WHAT HAPPENED AT GOLGOTHA?

- The reference to Pilate anchors the suffering of Jesus in history. When we discuss the crucifixion, we are dealing not with some fairy tale, but with an actual occurrence, a datable event.

- Adults need to understand the magnitude of suffering Jesus endured for his people, but we will need to use discretion as we describe crucifixion to the children under our care. Particulars of Roman crucifixion, such as the use of nails to hang the victim on the cross, may or may not be shared. The pivotal point to emphasize at this stage is that Christ actually suffered and died.

- But Christianity is not merely about the historical fact that Jesus Christ died on a cross; essentially, it is about the wonderful truth that Christ died *so that we can be forgiven.*

THE DILEMMA OF OUR PARDON: WHY CAN'T GOD JUST FORGIVE US?

- Since Genesis 3, a terrible conflict has existed between God and humanity, and Jesus is the only one who can put an end to this conflict.

- We are unable to repair our relationship with God, not only because we are enslaved to sin and therefore do not desire intimacy with God, but also because we have sinned against God and therefore only God can forgive and restore us.

- The Bible teaches us that God is loving and merciful, but also that he is holy and just. Because God is holy, he despises sin; our sin provokes his wrath.

- The appropriate punishment for sin is death, physical as well as spiritual, loss of the body as well as eternal separation from the loving and life-giving presence of God.

- The dilemma of our forgiveness: Confronted by human evil, how could God be true to himself as both loving and holy? He could not both pardon and punish us. God remained true to himself by punishing his appointed substitute so that his love could be directed toward us in forgiveness.

- This idea of *substitution* is introduced in the Old Testament sacrificial system. The Old Testament sacrifices pointed out the way of salvation, but the sacrifices themselves had no saving power.

THE PERFECT SUBSTITUTE: WHAT IS THE *MEANING* OF THE CROSS AND THE EMPTY TOMB?

- The death of Jesus is the sacrifice that accomplished what the Old Testament sacrifices pointed to but could not do.

- Jesus lived a life of perfect obedience, fulfilling God's righteous requirements for us, and he died the death of a sinner, absorbing God's holy hostility for us. Jesus is the Wrath-Quencher, the Anger-Eraser.

- Jesus is the sufferer of Good Friday, the proclaimer of Holy Saturday, and the victor of Easter Sunday.

- The resurrection is the revelation of the Father's acceptance of the life and death of Jesus as full and sufficient sacrifice.

- With the resurrection, we are assured that our fellowship with God is restored, and we are assured that death will not be the end for us. All those who believe in Christ will one day be raised bodily just as Christ himself was raised.

- Child-friendly summary of the truths discussed in this chapter: Jesus died on the cross for our sins and was raised on the third day, and when we believe this, we are forgiven of our sins and become forever friends with God.

Questions for the Family

Use these questions to spark discussion during your family worship times:

THE EVENT OF THE CRUCIFIXION: WHAT HAPPENED AT GOLGOTHA?

- Who was Pontius Pilate, and why is he mentioned in the Creed?

- Is it possible that Jesus just pretended to be dead? How do we know that he actually died?

THE DILEMMA OF OUR PARDON: WHY CAN'T GOD JUST FORGIVE US?

- What do we mean when we say that God is *holy*? How must the Holy God respond to sin?

- What do the Old Testament sacrifices teach us about *substitution*? Did these sacrifices have saving power?

THE PERFECT SUBSTITUTE: WHAT IS THE *MEANING* OF THE CROSS AND THE EMPTY TOMB?

- What do we mean when we say that Jesus is our *substitute*? Why did Jesus need to die for us?

- What happened on Holy Saturday and Easter Sunday?

- What does Jesus' death and bodily resurrection mean for those who believe in him?

Songs That Celebrate These Truths

As you study the truths summarized in part three of the Creed, also celebrate these truths as a family. Sing the following songs together, and try to memorize at least the first verse of each one.

- "It Is Well with My Soul"

- "Christ Arose"

Prayer Prompts

Always conclude your family worship times with prayer. Here are some prayer themes to keep in mind while your family studies this part of the Creed:

- God's holiness

- God's great love, demonstrated in the sending of his Son to be our substitute

- The victory of Jesus over sin, evil, and death

- The forgiveness of sin and fellowship with God that begins *now* and lasts *forever* for all those who believe in Jesus

4

The Son's Present Ministry and Second Coming

*He ascended into heaven and is seated at the right
hand of the Father. He will come again
to judge the living and the dead.*

*I believe in ... the resurrection of the body,
and the life everlasting. Amen.*

THE NEW CREATION AND THE SHARK WHO ATE ME

In the previous chapter, I claimed that heaven is *not* the ultimate hope of the Christ-follower. I suspect this assertion is
off-putting for some readers, but if you'll venture with me for
the duration of this chapter, you will see that the biblical hope
involves something far greater than heaven. This is not to suggest that heaven will be a letdown. Going to heaven won't be

like taking a trip to Lubbock, Texas. I once saw a funeral urn with an engraving that said, *I'd rather be here than in Lubbock.* You'll hear no objection from me. Far from being a disappointment, heaven is a place of great joy, of rest, and as we will see, a place of *waiting.* The final destination of the Christian is the new heaven and new earth, or what we might call the radically renovated creation.[1]

In the Thornton house, we talk often about the new creation. From our conversations spring all sorts of questions and imaginative ideas. Once my older son, Aidan, asked, "In the new creation, will I be able to drink as much as I want before bedtime without having to worry about peeing in the bed?" Presently my boys are most excited about the fact that in the new creation they will get to see a real Tyrannosaurus rex... and not have to worry about being eaten. As we were driving down the road one day, my younger son, Cullen, inquired, "Dad, will we get along with all animals in the new creation?" To which I replied, "Yes, son, we will." Immediately, he shouted: "Great! That means that if I get eaten by a shark on this earth, then when we get to the new earth, I can hunt down that shark and say, 'Hey, you ate me. But now we can be friends.'" Apparently my children spend a vast amount of time thinking about being eaten.

Having explored Jesus' identity, his birth (but not his beginning!), and his substitutionary death and bodily resurrection, we will now look at Jesus' return trip to heaven, commonly called *the ascension*. Jesus Christ is not only the risen Lord; he is also the ascended Lord. We'll need to consider what exactly this means for us and for our children. Additionally, the ascended Lord will one day descend, coming back to transform the earth and our mode of existence, putting an end to all suffering, setting all things right. Though Scripture reveals certain details about Christ's return, there are some things that God has decided not to disclose to us. When studying and teaching the doctrine of the second coming of Christ, we must heed the words of Deuteronomy 29:29: "The secret things belong to the LORD our God, but the revealed things belong to us and to our children forever."

THE APPEARANCE AND DISAPPEARANCE OF JESUS: UNDERSTANDING THE ASCENSION

The fourth part of the Apostles' Creed begins, "He ascended into heaven and is seated at the right hand of the Father." The account of Jesus' ascension is found in Acts 1. Luke, the author of Acts, begins the book by telling us that after Jesus was crucified, he presented himself alive to the disciples "by many convincing proofs."[2] The disciples had to be persuaded that Jesus had been raised from the dead. At the end of his first book, the Gospel of Luke, Luke tells us about these "convincing proofs."

In Luke 24, a group of women go to the tomb where Jesus had been buried, but when they arrive, they discover that the body is gone. Angels appear and announce, "Why do you look for the living among the dead? He is not here, but has risen." The women rush to the eleven disciples who are gathered with other followers of Jesus and relay the message: "Jesus is alive!" But the disciples don't believe it. Eventually, Jesus himself shows up in the house where the disciples are meeting, but even this isn't enough evidence for them. When he first appears, the disciples think they're seeing a ghost. So Jesus says, "Touch me. Feel that I am real. Feel my flesh and bones." But still the disciples remain unconvinced. Finally, Jesus asks them for fish, and he eats it in front of them. I imagine they asked him to eat several fish. Jesus probably didn't want fish again for a long time. All of this the Son of God did to prove to his disciples that he was, in fact, alive.

I'm a full-time pastor, so very few of my days are spent in the seclusion of a library working on books. The lion's share of

my time is spent with people, doing things like teaching, pray-
ing, mentoring, counseling, and having good old-fashioned
conversations. Not long ago I was having coffee with a man
who has attended our church for a while, though he doesn't
identify himself as a Christian. Somehow the subject of our
conversation shifted to the resurrection, and he confessed to
me that it is "this part of Christianity" with which he struggles
the most. "I believe in Jesus," he said, "but I'm not sure about
the resurrection part. I'm not sure we can trust the accounts we
find in the Gospels." This is a fairly common objection. Luke
tells us that the resurrected Jesus appeared to the disciples, but
how do we know we can trust Luke?

I can think of at least two reasons why we should read
Luke's account as reliable. First, remember that in Luke 24,
women are the first ones to bear witness to Jesus' resurrection.
In the ancient world, the testimony of a woman was admitted
in court or any sort of official setting only as a last resort. The
first-century historian Josephus refers to women as giddy or
frivolous, and therefore as unfit to serve as witnesses.[3] I'm
guessing this dude didn't get many dates. In a world where
women were considered to be unsuitable witnesses, no one
would have fabricated a story where the key witnesses were
women. Luke's account of the resurrection is so ridiculous that

it must be true. A second reason to trust Luke's account is the disbelief of the disciples. Think about everything I just summarized from Luke 24. In the narrative, the disciples are pictured as doubters, as people who are very slow to believe. If you're inventing a story that you hope will inspire countless followers of a new religious movement, you don't make the first followers look bad. You make them look clever, tenacious, and heroic. These details of the resurrection narrative—the presence of the women and the disbelief of the disciples—make no sense at all, unless the story is true. Unless Luke's account is accurate. Unless Jesus really is alive.

Returning to Acts 1, Luke explains that the risen Jesus remained with his disciples for forty days. At the end of this time, he told them to camp out in Jerusalem and wait for God's empowering presence, the Holy Spirit. "When the Spirit comes," Jesus said to them, "you will be my witnesses in Jerusalem, in all Judea and Samaria, and to the ends of the earth."[4] After he said these words, Jesus disappeared. Luke puts it like this: "When he had said this, as they were watching, he was lifted up, and a cloud took him out of their sight. While he was going and they were gazing up toward heaven, suddenly two men in white robes stood by them. They said, 'Men of Galilee, why do you stand looking up toward heaven? This Jesus, who has been taken up from you into heaven, will come in the same way as you saw him go into heaven.' "[5] As we teach our children about Jesus, we must emphasize his substitutionary death and bodily resurrection, but we mustn't stop there. We must remember that Jesus is not only the risen Lord, but also the ascended Lord. Jesus' ascension means at least three things for us and for our children: authority, advocacy, and intimacy.

First, the ascension means authority. Though Jesus has the ability to appear in some way to people on earth—such as Paul on the road to Damascus and John on the island of Patmos—the Creed affirms that he is "seated at the right hand of the Father."[6] This confirms Jesus' unique status. Not even the angels are allowed to sit at the Father's right hand, because this is the place of highest honor, the seat of shared authority.[7] Jesus came down to earth from heaven in great humility, and now he has returned to heaven in triumph and glory.[8] Having accomplished all that was necessary for our salvation, he now sits "far above all rule and authority and power and dominion, and above every name that is named."[9] Whatever our children are facing in life—difficult people, problems at school, physical or emotional pain—we must teach them to take the matter to Jesus, for he is the loving King with imponderable power.[10]

Second, the ascension means advocacy. When Jesus

ascended into heaven, he took his humanity with him. The incarnation is the once and for all union of God and man in the one person of Jesus, so the ascension is simply the relocation of this union—from earth to heaven.[11] By entering God's abode as the God-man, Jesus prepares the way for us. But Jesus didn't open heaven for us and then take a seat to have a snooze. Christ is seated in heaven, but he is not *at rest*; he is still *at work*. What is he doing? He has the Father's ear.[12] Jesus appears before the Father as our advocate. John Calvin writes, "He appears before the Father's face as our constant advocate and intercessor.... Thus he turns the Father's eyes to his own righteousness to avert his gaze from our sin."[13] What Calvin means is that Christ uses his sinless life and sacrificial death on the cross as the plea for the Father to forgive the sins we *continue to commit*.[14]

Here it is helpful to remember that the resurrected body of Christ continues to bear the marks of his suffering and death.[15] I have a small scar on the side of my head, just above my left ear. I wish I could say that there's a thrilling, manly tale behind my scar, something like the shark attack stories Quint and Hooper share in *Jaws*. But the truth evokes no admiration: a rusty fishing lure got stuck in the side of my melon. Still, the scar works well for the purpose of pointing my boys to scars that are infinitely more impressive. "See Daddy's scar, boys?

It never goes away. Jesus' scars will never go away either. He's sitting in heaven right now, and every time you sin, he points to his scars, looks to God the Father, and says, 'I died for that.' " Our children need to know that they don't have to worry about losing their salvation. They don't have to hit the pillow at night wondering if they've done something in the course of the day that has caused the Father to reject them. *Christ remains in himself our eternal security.* The embodied communion between God and man, the one who died to reconcile us to the Father, sits on his throne with the scars that prove we will never bear the punishment for our sin.[16]

Third, the ascension means greater intimacy with Jesus. As you read this, your first thought might be something like, "How can this be the case, since Jesus has disappeared from view?" I agree with you that at first this seems a strange conclusion to draw from the ascension. I don't tend to feel closer to my wife and boys when I'm in Providence, Rhode Island, speaking at a conference and they're back home in Seminole, Florida. What makes Jesus' departure from us different? In John 20 the risen Jesus appears to Mary Magdalene. Mary is weeping because she thinks Jesus is dead and thus gone forever. When Jesus appears, Mary is so overjoyed that she grabs him and refuses to let go. Jesus says to her, "Mary, don't cling to me.

Let me ascend." What is Jesus doing here? In essence, he's saying, "Mary, if I stay here on the earth, sooner or later, you'll have to let go of me. You'll need to eat. You'll need to sleep. You can't hold my hand forever! So let me ascend and send the Holy Spirit to you, and through him I will be present with you always." This is precisely what happens in Acts 2. After Jesus *ascends*, the Spirit *descends* to indwell believers. This doesn't mean that the Son went to heaven, was transformed into the Holy Spirit, and then descended to indwell us. Remember our key terms of triune thinking from Chapter 1: unity, equality, and *distinguishability*. Jesus is not the Holy Spirit. Rather, it means that the Holy Spirit is the bond who unites us to the ascended Jesus so that wherever we go, the all-powerful, world-ruling King actually is present with us.

THE UNCERTAINTY OF JESUS' REAPPEARANCE

The risen and ascended Lord is also the *returning* Lord. On the day of Jesus' ascension, the angels declared, "This Jesus, who has been taken up from you into heaven, will come in the same way as you saw him go into heaven."[17] The fourth part of the Apostles' Creed says, "He will come again to judge the living and the dead," and the Creed concludes with the words,

"I believe in...the resurrection of the body, and the life ever-lasting. Amen." With these words we come to the bewildering field of *eschatology*, which technically refers to the study of "last things," though I prefer to think of it as the study of *the Christian hope*.[18]

Before we became Floridians, my family spent a few years ministering in Colorado. When we first moved to Colorado, we took some time to find a new family doctor and a new dentist. The dentist we settled on was great. Friendly people. Massage chairs. Very little flak about insufficient flossing. What more could a guy ask for? But when I first saw my new dentist, he asked me the strangest question: "What are your goals for your teeth?" I had never thought about my "goals for my teeth," so I just said the first thing that came to mind: "I guess I'd like to keep them." He responded, "Well, that's a modest goal. I think we can handle that."

You should know that my goal in this section is indeed a modest one. I will not attempt to answer every question you have about eschatology. I will not be sketching fantastic crea-tures or providing a detailed timeline of end-of-days events. Sorry to disappoint. My goal, simply stated, is to summarize the firm hope of Christianity. And by "firm," I mean both cer-tain/definite and solid/physical.

As we enter the arena of eschatology, we must first admit what we do *not* know. The most important admission is that we do not know *when* Christ will return. On the one hand, we can say that we are closer to the second coming of Christ than ever before. But on the other hand, we must admit that no one knows how much longer it will be. Jesus makes this clear just before he ascends into heaven. The disciples ask him if the time has come for him to establish his earthly kingdom. Jesus responds not by denying the reality that he will one day establish an earthly kingdom, but by saying, "It is not for you to know the times or periods that the Father has set by his own authority."[19] Jesus will one day return to earth. This much is *certain*. But the timing of Christ's return is *uncertain* to everyone except the Father himself. In Matthew 24:36–44, Jesus says:

> But about that day and hour no one knows, neither the angels of heaven, nor the Son, but only the Father. For as the days of Noah were, so will be the coming of the Son of Man. For as in those days before the flood they were eating and drinking, marrying and giving in marriage, until the day Noah entered the ark, and they knew nothing until the flood came and swept them all away, so too will be the coming of the Son of Man. Then two will be in the field; one will

be taken and one will be left. Two women will be grinding meal together; one will be taken and one will be left. Keep awake therefore, for you do not know on what day your Lord is coming. But understand this: if the owner of the house had known in what part of the night the thief was coming, he would have stayed awake and would not have let his house be broken into. Therefore you also must be ready, for the Son of Man is coming at an unexpected hour.

Emphatic in this passage is the idea that the unpredictability of Jesus' return should lead to a perpetual readiness among Christians. We cannot possibly know when the Son will come again; therefore, we must always be prepared. If I order something on Amazon, and I know it's going to be delivered on Thursday, then I don't look for it on Tuesday. We don't have a tracking number on Jesus. We don't know exactly when he will arrive, and so we should be longing for his return and living for him every day.

Countless Christians throughout history have chosen to ignore the fact that Jesus is "untrackable." In the nineteenth century, a man named William Miller thought he had figured out exactly when Jesus was going to return. March 21, 1843, was the day he predicted. March 21 came, but Jesus didn't.

Convinced he had made a mathematical error, Miller recal-
culated and came up with a new date: October 22, 1844. On
October 22, roughly 100,000 Christians gathered and waited
for Christ's return. Everyone showed up at the party. Everyone
except the guest of honor; Jesus was a no-show. Fast-forward
over a century and we come to the former NASA engineer
Edgar Whisenant. Poor Edgar predicted the rapture of the
church would take place in 1988. His book, *88 Reasons Why
the Rapture Will Be in 1988*, sold over 4 million copies. Sad,
but true. The point to be made here is that Jesus himself doesn't
even know when he is returning to earth, and any person who
thinks he knows more than Jesus is a fool, and should be treated
as such.

As I've said before, children of faith need the diet of doctrine, but not all doctrine is healthy! Parent-theologians are
called to prepare and serve truth in the home, but we must also
protect against false teaching. It's one thing for me to serve my
children a plate of grilled chicken, sweet potatoes, and green
beans. It's something else for me to teach them to stay away
from toxic chemicals in the garage. If we're concerned about
the health of our children, both *preparing* and *protecting* are
important. And if we take the protecting task seriously, there
will be occasions when we will need to say to our children, "I

don't want you to read this book." Or maybe we read the book with them and help them see how the message it communicates is unbiblical. It is always necessary to test the texts and teachers before us, even if they are found in the Christian section of the bookstore or on a Christian channel. Jesus himself said, "Beware of false prophets, who come to you in sheep's clothing but inwardly are ravenous wolves."[20] Wolves have pens. And producers.

In addition to the timing of Christ's return, there are other eschatological matters that remain cryptic, and some of these are fiercely debated. Someone once said that the "millennium," which is spoken of in Revelation 20, is the thousand years of peace that Christians like to fight over. When does this thousand-year period occur? Is it a literal thousand-year period? Believers answer these questions in a variety of ways. We have the amillennials, the premillennials, and the postmillennials, all of whom get their name from the Book of Revelation. But as the nineteenth-century writer Ambrose Bierce once said, Revelation is "a famous book in which St. John the Divine concealed all that he knew. The revealing is done by the commentators, who know nothing."[21] Without becoming distracted by the minutiae, the Apostles' Creed points us to the essentials of eschatology: Christ's visible, bodily return to judge the living and the dead, and everlasting, bodily life for all those who belong to Christ. On these points, all Christians agree.

THE REALITY OF RESURRECTION

James tells us that earthly life is like a mist that appears for a short time and then vanishes.[22] God gives us only this fleeting time on earth to respond to the gospel.[23] As we learned in Chapter 3, Jesus has accomplished our salvation. He lived a life of perfect obedience, fulfilling God's righteous requirements for us, and he died the death of a sinner, absorbing God's holy hostility for us. But what Jesus has *accomplished for us* is not *applied to us* until we place our faith in him. In the words of John 3:36, "Whoever believes in the Son has eternal life; whoever does not obey the Son shall not see life, but the wrath of God remains on him."[24] At the second coming, all people—"the living and the dead"—will be judged on the basis of their response to Jesus Christ. This should be understood as a strong warning to those who ignore the Son of God. But the final judgment should bring joy to the hearts of those who acknowledge Christ as Lord. As Karl Barth says, "We have no reason to fear.... There is only one who might be against us: Jesus Christ. And it is he, precisely, who is for us!"[25] Jesus presently has the Father's ear for us, and when the judgment comes, Jesus will again speak on our behalf.

Before further exploring the events that will transpire at Christ's return, we should pause for a moment to consider what happens to believers who die prior to the second coming. Through time, the body becomes worn, ravaged, diseased, and dysfunctional to the point where the soul no longer can be expressed through it. Death is the separation of soul and body. When believers die, our bodies return to the dust, but our souls survive. The immaterial part of our person returns to the God who made it.[26] Reinhold Niebuhr once said that afterlife discussions often become preoccupied with such matters as "the furniture of heaven or the temperature of hell."[27] I don't know what type of furniture awaits us, but I do know that Paul speaks of life in heaven as being "far better" than life in the world as it is presently, full of sin and death.[28] However, it's important to remember that heaven is only *the intermediate state*—"better" but not "best." The words of the old song should be changed from "This world is not my home, I'm just passing through" to "*Heaven* is not my home, I'm just passing through." The ultimate hope of the Christian is the resurrection of the body and eternal life in the new world that Christ will bring when he returns. Parents, we must teach our children about the reality of resurrection, but this means that we must also teach them about the reality of death. There may not be a way to teach young children about death and resurrection without the discussion ending in tears. When I first explained the concepts to my boys (as we read the end of *The Silver Chair*, when Caspian dies), they both ended up crying. But much to my surprise, the next day my sons began using resurrection language in ways quite appropriate for a five- and a seven-year-old. "Dad, I'm not scared of dying. I'll come back to life just like Jesus did. I'll even have a new body. Dad, do you think I'll have a superhero body? Can I be Captain America?!"

Of all the New Testament texts dealing with Jesus' return, 1 Thessalonians 4:13–18 contains the most explicit description. Paul writes:

> But we do not want you to be uninformed, brothers and sisters, about those who have died, so that you may not grieve as others do who have no hope. For since we believe that Jesus died and rose again, even so, through Jesus, God will bring with him those who have died. For this we declare to you by the word of the Lord, that we who are alive, who are left until the coming of the Lord, will by no means precede those who have died. For the Lord himself, with a cry of

command, with the archangel's call and with the sound of
God's trumpet, will descend from heaven, and the dead in
Christ will rise first. Then we who are alive, who are left,
will be caught up in the clouds together with them to meet
the Lord in the air; and so we will be with the Lord forever.
Therefore encourage one another with these words.

In this passage, the pastoral Paul is writing to comfort believers in Thessalonica who are concerned about their loved ones who have passed away. "Don't worry about these deceased brothers and sisters," Paul proclaims, "because Christ died and rose again, and he will surely return." In verses 15–17, Paul clarifies three stages of Christ's second coming. First, Christ descends from heaven. This is the same Jesus—fully God and fully man—who ascended into heaven. It is a visible, bodily return of our Lord. Second, deceased Christians are resurrected. Those who have been in the presence of Jesus in heaven since their deaths will receive their new, imperishable bodies.[29] Third, living Christians are transformed, clothed with their new bodies, and all believers will join their Lord for eternity.[30]

Contrary to the popular assumption, verse 17 probably does not refer to a secret rapture of the church. Some find here a one-and-a-half coming of Christ; Jesus, like a ninja warrior, comes down to cloud level, snatches up all the believers, and then takes them back to heaven. True, the text does not tell us *where* believers go after they "meet the Lord in the air." But the word translated as "meet" is the Greek word *apantēsis*, a technical term for a well-known custom in the ancient world. The custom involved the sending of citizens outside the city to welcome a king or high-ranking official and to escort him on the final part of his journey. The idea in 1 Thessalonians 4 is that all Christians are taken up to meet their Lord in the air, and then we will accompany him as his entourage on the remainder of his victorious descent to earth. It is here *on the earth* that "we will always be with the Lord."

PLANET HEAVEN

But the earth will not be the same. When Jesus returns, he will renovate this world, transforming it into a kingdom fit for God. Planet earth will become planet heaven. We get a glimpse of this new world in Revelation 21:1–4:

Then I saw a new heaven and a new earth; for the first heaven and the first earth had passed away, and the sea was no more.[31] *And I saw the holy city, the new Jerusalem, coming down out of heaven from God, prepared as a bride adorned for her husband. And I heard a loud voice from the throne saying, "See, the home of God is among mortals. He will dwell with them as their God; they will be his peoples, and God himself will be with them; he will wipe every tear from their eyes. Death will be no more; mourning and crying and pain will be no more, for the first things have passed away."*

These first several verses announce the realities of the new creation, while the remaining verses of Revelation 21– 22 develop these realities in more detail. The pivotal thing to note is *the Easter pattern*, found in verse 1: the first creation "passes away" and is replaced by "a new heaven and a new earth." This is the death and resurrection pattern established by Christ himself. Jesus died and was raised. Jesus says to us, "I am the resurrection and the life. Those who believe in me, even though they die, will live."[32] And now we see in Revelation 21 that when Jesus returns, the first creation will pass away and a new creation will emerge. The first renovation of the world came by water.[33] Peter tells us that the final purification will occur by fire.[34] As we envision this purification of the earth, there are two errors we must avoid. Douglas Wilson writes,

"One mistake is that of thinking this creation will be burnt to a cinder and not replaced, or replaced by something completely unrelated. The other mistake is that of thinking that this creation will simply be tidied up a bit, with a certain amount of polish and shine. The Lord comes back with some touch-up paint, and regiments of angels scatter around the world to give our Botox treatments."[35]

The rescuing of this world from its current corruption will mean transformations we cannot fully fathom, but this redeeming work will not mean that God will say of space and matter, "Oh, well. Nice try. Good while it lasted."[36] The story of Scripture, and the story of the Apostles' Creed, runs from creation to new creation. God's people are promised a new type of *bodily* existence in a *physical* place for *all eternity.* As C. S. Lewis puts it, we will not be floating wraiths, but solid people, people who eat fish, cast shadows in the sunlight, and make a noise when we tramp the floor.[37] We should imagine bodies that are more solid than our present ones. We should envision an earth that is more magnificent.

One of the best things we can do to help our children understand the beauty and solidity of the new creation is to read the Chronicles of Narnia series with them. At the end of *The Last Battle*, the final volume of the series, C. S. Lewis describes the difference between the old Narnia and the new Narnia. He writes: "The new one was a deeper country: every rock and flower and blade of grass looked as if it meant more....It was the Unicorn who summed up what everyone was feeling. He stamped his right forehoof on the ground and neighed, and then cried: 'I have come home at last! This is my real country! I belong here. This is the land I have been looking for all my life, though I never knew it till now. *The reason why we loved the old Narnia is that it sometimes looked a little like this.*' "[38] The Christian hope is a cosmic hope. We long for the return of our Lord, the resurrection of the body, and the radical renovation of the entire world.

FAMILY WORSHIP GUIDE

The Apostles' Creed

As a family, memorize the fourth part of the Creed in two simple steps. We also covered the final words of the Creed in Chapter 4, but we'll wait until Chapter 6 to memorize that part.

> *He ascended into heaven and is seated at the right hand*
> *of the Father.*
> *He will come again to judge the living and the dead.*

Key Verses

In addition to memorizing the fourth part of the Creed, choose one or more of the following passages to treasure in your heart:

JESUS, OUR ADVOCATE

> *My dear children, I write this to you so that you will not sin. But if anybody does sin, we have an advocate with the Father—Jesus Christ, the Righteous One. (1 John 2:1 NIV)*

BEING READY FOR JESUS' RETURN

> *So you also must be ready, because the Son of Man will come at an hour when you do not expect him. (Matthew 24:44 NIV)*

BODILY RESURRECTION

For the Lord himself will come down from heaven, with a loud command, with the voice of the archangel and with the trumpet call of God, and the dead in Christ will rise first. After that, we who are still alive and are left will be caught up together with them in the clouds to meet the Lord in the air. And so we will be with the Lord forever. (1 Thessalonians 4:16–17 NIV)

THE NEW CREATION

And I heard a loud voice from the throne saying, "Look! God's dwelling place is now among the people, and he will dwell with them. They will be his people, and God himself will be with them and be their God. 'He will wipe every tear from their eyes. There will be no more death' or mourning or crying or pain, for the old order of things has passed away." (Revelation 21:3–4; Isaiah 25:8 NIV)

Nuggets of Truth

Parent-theologians, when teaching your children-disciples, be sure to cover these main points from Chapter 4:

THE APPEARANCE AND DISAPPEARANCE OF JESUS: UNDERSTANDING THE ASCENSION

- As we teach our children about Jesus, we must emphasize his substitutionary death and bodily resurrection, but we mustn't stop there. We must remember that Jesus is not only the risen Lord, but also the *ascended* Lord.

- Jesus' ascension means at least three things for us and for our children: *authority, advocacy, and intimacy.*

  ○ Authority: The Creed tells us that Jesus is "seated at the right hand of the Father." This confirms his unique status. Not even the angels are allowed to sit at the Father's right hand, because this is the place of highest honor, the seat of shared authority.

  ○ Advocacy: The ascended Jesus uses his sinless life and sacrificial death on the cross as the plea for the Father to forgive the sins we continue to commit. Jesus sits on his throne with the scars that prove we will never bear the punishment for our sin.

  ○ Intimacy: When Jesus ascended, the Holy Spirit descended to live inside believers. The Spirit is the bond who unites us to the ascended Jesus so that wherever we go, the all-powerful, world-ruling King Jesus is present with us.

THE UNCERTAINTY OF JESUS' REAPPEARANCE

- The risen and ascended Lord is also the *returning* Lord.

- Jesus will one day return to earth. This much is certain. But the timing of Christ's return is uncertain to everyone except the Father himself.

- Because we don't know exactly when Jesus will reappear, we should live for him every day.

- Some people have tried to predict when Jesus will return, but the Bible clearly teaches us that no person is privy to this information.

- Children of faith need the diet of doctrine, but not all doctrine is healthy. Parents are called to prepare and serve truth in the home, but we must also protect against false teaching. It is always necessary to test the texts and teachers before us, even if they are found in the Christian section of the bookstore or on a Christian channel.

THE REALITY OF RESURRECTION

- What Jesus has accomplished for us is not applied to us until we place our faith in him. At the second coming, all people—"the living and the dead"—will be judged on the basis of their response to Jesus Christ.

- Death is the separation of soul and body. When believers die, our bodies return to the dust, but our souls survive in heaven.

- The Bible teaches us that life in heaven is "far better" than life in the world as it is presently, full of sin and death. However, it's important to remember that heaven is only the intermediate state—"better" but not "best."

- The ultimate hope of the Christian is the resurrection of the body and eternal life in the new world that Christ will bring when he returns.

PLANET HEAVEN

- When Jesus returns, he will renovate this world, transforming it into a kingdom fit for God. Planet earth will become planet heaven.

- God's people are promised a new type of bodily existence in a physical place for all eternity. We should imagine bodies that are more solid than our present ones. We should envision an earth that is more magnificent.

Questions for the Family

Use these questions to spark discussion during your family worship times:

THE APPEARANCE AND DISAPPEARANCE OF JESUS: UNDERSTANDING THE ASCENSION

- After Jesus was raised from the dead, what did he do? Where did he go?

- When the Bible and the Apostles' Creed talk about Jesus being "seated at the right hand of the Father," what does this mean? Why is he seated at the "right hand"?

- Is the ascended Jesus still fully God and fully man? Does he still bear the marks of the crucifixion? What do the scars of Jesus teach us?

- Through the Holy Spirit, the all-powerful King is present with us always. What are some of our fears or worries that we should take to King Jesus?

THE UNCERTAINTY OF JESUS' REAPPEARANCE

- The Bible and the Apostles' Creed teach us that Jesus will one day return to earth. Is there a way for us to figure out *when* he will return?

- Since we can't possibly determine when Jesus will return, we should be ready for his return every day. What does it mean to be *ready* for the second coming?

- How should we respond to people who think they have figured out when Jesus is returning?

THE REALITY OF RESURRECTION

- When Jesus returns, he will "judge the living and the dead." What does this mean?

- What will happen to those who believe in Jesus when they die?

- What do you think life in heaven will be like?

- What will happen to believers when Jesus returns?

PLANET HEAVEN

- What do you think the new creation (planet heaven) will be like?

Songs That Celebrate These Truths

As you study the truths summarized in part four of the Creed, also celebrate these truths as a family. Sing the following songs together, and try to memorize at least the first verse of each one.

- "Crown Him with Many Crowns"

- "Christ the Lord Is Risen Today"

Prayer Prompts

Always conclude your family worship times with prayer. Here are some prayer themes to keep in mind while your family studies this part of the Creed:

- Jesus, the King of all creation and our Advocate in heaven

- The certainty of Jesus' return

- Being ready for Jesus' return/serving him faithfully each day

- Heaven as a place of joy, rest, and waiting

- The ultimate hope of bodily resurrection and eternal life in the new creation

5
The Holy Spirit

I believe in the Holy Spirit.

KILLING THE HEAVENLY BUZZ

In this chapter, we'll rewind to the interval between Jesus' ascension and his return, the interval of our existence. The New Testament refers to this period of time as "the last days." In the first Christian sermon, preached on the Day of Pentecost, the Apostle Peter quotes the Prophet Joel, saying, "In the last days it will be, God declares, *that I will pour out my Spirit upon all flesh.*"[1] Of the three persons of the Trinity, the Holy Spirit is the one most misunderstood. As one biblical scholar puts it, "I say with no exaggeration that I have met Christians who seem to think of the Holy Spirit as something like Jesus's vapor trail, or a mysterious and impersonal 'force' that conveys God's presence, or even a kind of heavenly buzz that falls on people when some funky psychedelic worship music is played. The way some people describe the Holy Spirit could just as well describe magnetism, mood rings, or Motown records from the 1960s."[2] We need to begin by killing the idea of the Spirit as a force or heavenly buzz. If we switch to an athletic image, the Holy Spirit is less like the preworkout supplement you drink to give you energy (a *substance*) and more like the coach or trainer pushing you on (a *person*).[3] The Holy Spirit is not an *it*; the Holy Spirit is a *he*.

After establishing the identity of the Spirit, we'll need to think about the activity of the Spirit. In short, the Bible teaches us that the Holy Spirit brings us into personal fellowship with Christ, guides us to an understanding of Christ's teaching, and empowers us to do Christ's work in the world. Notice the emphasis I'm placing on the Holy Spirit *pointing us to Christ*. The Spirit "demonstrates profound boldness in promoting another, Jesus Christ."[4] J. I. Packer writes, "The Spirit's message to us is never, 'Look at me; listen to me; come to me; get to know me,' but always, 'Look at *him*, and see his glory; listen to *him*, and hear his word; go to *him*, and have life; get to know *him*, and taste his gift of joy and peace.'"[5] The most fundamental point about the activity of the Holy Spirit is that his is "a flood-light ministry." Floodlights throw light on a building while remaining hidden themselves. If the lights are placed properly, you don't notice them at all. What you're meant to see is the building, on which the lights are trained. The intended effect is to make the building visible, when otherwise it would be lost in the darkness of the night, and to maximize its beauty and dignity.[6] This, in a nutshell, is the ministry of the Holy Spirit, the third person of the Trinity. He is "the hidden floodlight shining on the Savior."[7]

HE WHO IS GOD

In Chapter 1, we talked about the importance of thinking rightly about our triune God. Christians affirm the *three-in-oneness* of God. Though there is only one true God, this God eternally exists as three distinct persons. In the words of the Apostles' Creed: "I believe in *God, the Father almighty*...I believe in *Jesus Christ*, his only Son, our Lord...and I believe in *the Holy Spirit*." In Acts 5, the Apostle Peter explicitly refers to the Holy Spirit as God. Ananias and Sapphira, a husband and wife, decided to sell a piece of their property and give the proceeds to the work of gospel ministry, but Ananias became greedy and stashed some of the money for himself. When Peter found out about this, he confronted Ananias: "Why has Satan filled your heart to lie to the Holy Spirit and to keep back part of the pro-ceeds of the land?" Peter goes on to say, "How is it that you have contrived this deed in your heart? You did not lie to us but to *God*!"[8] Acts 5 most clearly uses the language of "God" in reference to the Holy Spirit, but the early church nearly always thought of the final verses of Matthew's Gospel as the most unmistakable affirmation of the Spirit's deity. According to Matthew 28:19, we are to baptize "in the name [singular] of the Father and of the Son and of the Holy Spirit." Here and in the other trinitarian expressions of the New Testament, the Holy Spirit is classified on an equal level with God the Father and God the Son. It would have been unthinkable for Jesus to say something like, "Baptize in the name of the Father and of the Son and of the Apostle Paul or the archangel Michael," for this would categorize a created being with the uncreated Father and Son. Believers throughout the ages can be baptized only in the name of God himself: Father, Son, and Holy Spirit.[9]

Scripture is clear that the Holy Spirit is fully God, the third person of the Trinity, but what do we mean when we say that the *Spirit* is a *person*? The word "person" is potentially mis-leading. When we say that God eternally exists in three distinct persons, we do not mean that he exists as three *human beings* or that he has *three bodies*. The incarnate Son has a body—he is the God-*man*—but the Father and the Spirit do not. We can ask how much the Son weighs, how tall he is, and what size running shoe he wears, but we cannot ask these questions of the Spirit. What exactly do we mean, then, when we say that the Holy Spirit is a person? We mean that the Spirit, like the Father and the Son, is able to give and receive love. The Spirit is not an impersonal force. As we will see, the Spirit leads us, speaks to us, and gives gifts to us. And perhaps most relevant for the present discussion, the Spirit can experience grief: "And do not grieve the Holy Spirit of God, with which you were marked with a seal for the day of redemption."[10] A person suffers grief; a puff of smoke does not.[11]

As the third person of the Trinity, the Spirit has always existed and has always been at work in the world. Many believers tend to think of Pentecost (Acts 2) as the Spirit's first rodeo, but this is not so. The Spirit was there at the beginning, "hovering over the face of the waters."[12] In the Old Testament, the Holy Spirit empowered people for special service, such as Joshua, Ezekiel, and Micah, to name just a few.[13] The Gospels report the descent of the Holy Spirit on the Son at his baptism.[14] So we must affirm the existence and activity of the Spirit prior to Acts 2. But we must also acknowledge that the Holy Spirit comes *in a new way* in Acts 2, the way promised in Ezekiel 36:27: "And I will put my Spirit *within you*, and cause you to walk in my statutes and be careful to obey my rules."[15] On the Day of Pentecost, the Holy Spirit comes to indwell believers, making a permanent home in their hearts.[16]

HE WHO GIVES LIFE

Ezekiel 36 indicates that the Spirit is the one who enables us to walk in the ways of the Lord. To fully understand this assertion, we need to return to the doctrine of original sin.[17]

As descendants of Adam, all human beings are sinful or corrupt to the very core of our being. In our natural state, we are unable to please God.[18] Another way to put this is to say, as Paul does in Ephesians 2:1, that we are *spiritually dead*. In John 3, we read about a Pharisee named Nicodemus. On a dark and stormy night, Nicodemus approaches Jesus. In the midst of their conversation, Jesus says something peculiar. "Very truly, I tell you, no one can see the kingdom of God without being born from above." Nicodemus immediately replies, "How can anyone be born after having grown old? Can one enter a second time into the mother's womb and be born?" Jesus explains, "No one can enter the kingdom of God without being born of water and *Spirit*." When Jesus says that we need to be "born from above," or as other translations put it, "born again," he is referring to spiritual birth; he means that we need to be made spiritually alive. The image of birth is telling. How much say did you have in your physical birth? Not a bit. You didn't choose to be born physically, and you cannot simply choose to be born spiritually. Thus, the predicament we find ourselves in is that this new birth of which Jesus speaks is *something that everyone needs*, but it is also *something that no one can achieve*.

Enter the Holy Spirit, the power of our second birth, the giver of spiritual life.[19] Since we are unable to revive ourselves, the Spirit breathes new life into our spiritual corpses. In theological terms, this is the sovereign and gracious work of *regeneration*. The Holy Spirit brings us to life, changing the sinful heart, so that we are able to respond to God in faith and repentance.[20] As I've said before, what Christ has accomplished for us is not applied to us until we place our faith in him. Martin Luther says, "Of what help is it to you that God is God, if he is not *God to you*?"[21] Or as John Calvin puts it, "As long as Christ remains outside of us, and we are separated from him, all that he has suffered and done for the salvation of the human race remains useless and of no value for us."[22] The Holy Spirit is the one who unites us to Christ, providing access to everything the Son has done for us. That we may become *partakers* of the salvation Christ has *purchased* for us, the Spirit regenerates us and gives us the gift of faith.

If the Spirit is indeed the giver of spiritual life and saving faith, then this means that the analogy of salvation I've heard various preachers use throughout my life doesn't really work. The analogy goes something like this: "You're in the middle of the ocean of sin, struggling to stay afloat, and your strength is quickly failing. You've gone under twice and bobbed back to the surface, and if you go under once more, you will be doomed. But if you'll reach out and take Jesus' hand, he will save you." The problem with this illustration is that it both *overestimates* the human condition and *underestimates* God's work. According to Scripture, we're not drowning. We're already stone cold dead, dead in our trespasses and sins.[23] And Jesus doesn't reach out his hand, gesturing for us to come to him. The Holy Spirit comes to us on the ocean floor, he breathes life into us, lifts us out of the depths, and unites us with Jesus. The gospel is not about God asking bad people to become good. It's about the gracious God making dead people alive. It's not about God lending a hand to someone who is struggling. It's about the sovereign God reviving a corpse!

Thus far we've determined that the Holy Spirit is the giver of life and faith, but what exactly is faith, and how do we know when it is present in our children? Here, again, Calvin is helpful. He defines faith as a fiery certainty, a deep-seated knowledge of God's love toward us, demonstrated in the sending of the Son on our behalf. This knowledge, Calvin says, is both "revealed to our *minds* and sealed upon our *hearts* through the Holy Spirit."[24] Faith, then, is cognitive; it involves a mental acceptance of Jesus Christ as he is offered to us in the gospel. But true faith, saving faith, is more than cognitive. It's also affective and behavioral; with faith comes new attitudes, desires, and conduct. Remember that there can be no genuine faith without the work of the Spirit, and the Spirit is the *Holy* Spirit, the *Sanctifying* Spirit; thus, it follows that with faith comes a devout disposition.[25] As Paul says, "If anyone is in Christ, there is a new creation."[26]

Every time I read this Pauline text, I think of a story from the life of Augustine, the famous fourth-century theologian. The story is perhaps apocryphal, but it's a powerful illustration nonetheless. Augustine was the son of a pagan father named Patricius and a Christian mother named Monica. In his years as a student, Augustine lived a promiscuous life. If we transported him from the fourth century to the present day, we would probably refer to him as a sex addict. In his spiritual autobiography, *Confessions*, Augustine refers to himself as "a slave of lust." When he tells of his conversion, he describes it as the story of how God "delivered me from the chain of sexual desire, by which I was tightly bound."[27] Sometime after his conversion, Augustine came across a woman with whom he formerly had an intense sexual relationship. She was friendly and flirtatious, probably expecting things to pick up right where they had left them. But Augustine paid no attention to the woman; he simply kept walking down the street. Worried that Augustine had not recognized her, the former mistress cried out, "Augustine, it is I!" Augustine turned back to the woman and replied, "I know, but it is not I."

"If anyone is in Christ, there is a new creation."[28] The Holy Spirit brings about this new creation. We are brought from death to life, and our born-again identity will become increasingly evident in our conversations and conduct. The same will be true of our children. Unfortunately, this doesn't mean that once our children have saving faith, they will grow halos, call a permanent truce with their siblings, and perfectly obey their parents. I wish. No, the children of God are freed from the bondage to sin, but not yet freed from sin itself. "The Spirit dispenses a power whereby they may gain the upper hand and become victors in the struggle. But sin ceases only to reign; it does not also cease to dwell in them."[29] What we're looking for in our children is *struggle against sin*, or what might be called *progressive sanctification*. We're not looking for *sinless perfection*. We'll come back to the idea of sanctification in the next section. But before moving on, I want to issue a warning concerning how parents and children's workers sometimes give children a false sense of security regarding salvation.

Many years ago I served as a children's pastor. One day we had a guest speaker in children's chapel who—with good intentions, I'm sure—did something that I consider to be extremely harmful. After giving his Bible talk, he concluded by saying to a room full of preschool and elementary kids, "Now, raise your hand if you want to go to heaven." Of course, every hand in the room went up. The speaker then proceeded to have the children repeat after him what he called "the sinner's prayer." This was followed by the pronouncement, "And now you're all saved!" I had to spend the next several weeks cleaning up the mess this well-meaning but theologically uninformed brother left behind.[30]

I hope you immediately sense the problems with this

gentleman's approach, but just in case you don't, I'll explain why this sort of thing is extremely harmful to our children. First, the speaker did not take the time to ensure that each child in the room had an age-appropriate understanding of the gospel. We must remember that there is a cognitive element to genuine faith. The Holy Spirit "reveals to our minds" the truth of the gospel.[31] It simply will not do to ask our children, "Do you want to go to heaven?" This question tells us absolutely nothing about their understanding of the person and work of Christ. A far better question is, "What do you believe about Jesus?" Second, while the Bible *does* declare that authentic conversion involves a confession of the lips, it *does not* provide us with a formulaic prayer that must be prayed. It is misleading to speak of "the sinner's prayer" as some magical expression that guarantees salvation. This brings me to my third objection, which is that though authentic conversion involves verbal confession, it cannot be reduced to this. According to the Apostle Paul, "If you confess with your lips that Jesus is Lord *and believe in your heart* that God raised him from the dead, you will be saved."[32] Paul pictures a confessional commitment that flows from a transformed heart. The Holy Spirit brings us to life (regeneration), reveals to our minds and seals upon our hearts the truth of God's love for us (faith), and the result is that we forsake our sin and follow Jesus as Lord (repentance).

How, then, do we know if our children are genuine believers? The true test is not the utterance of a prayer, but the passage of time. To determine if a man is alive, you don't ask to see his birth certificate. You watch to see if he is breathing, moving, and walking presently. To determine if our children are spiritually alive, we don't flip to the front page of their Bibles looking for the dates they raised their hands in church or prayed a certain prayer. Rather, we examine the way they are living presently. Again, we're not looking for sinless perfection. Sin will remain in them, though it will not reign. If we see in our children a consistent struggle against sin, submission to God's authority, and love for God and others, then we can be certain that God has done a gracious and mighty work in them, and that they have eternal fellowship with him.[33]

HE WHO GUIDES AND EMPOWERS

Having seen how the Holy Spirit brings us into fellowship with Christ, we'll now think about the continuing activity of the Spirit in the life of the Christian. The Spirit is the revealer, teacher, and persuader who guides us to an understanding of Christ's teaching, and he is the empowering presence who enables us to do the work of Christ in the world. Several ideas need to be unpacked here. We should begin with the production of Scripture, or what is known as the doctrine of *inspiration*. The Holy Spirit guided the Old Testament and New Testament writers in such a way that with their human hands they wrote the very message of God.[34] The Apostle Peter tells us, "No prophecy ever came by human will, but men and women moved by the Holy Spirit spoke from God."[35] The Holy Spirit plays the pivotal role not only in the production of Scripture but also in our reception of Scripture.[36] This is commonly referred to as the Spirit's ministry of *illumination*; the Spirit brings light. It is the inward work of the Holy Spirit that enables us to welcome the Word of God, seeing the message as true and aligning ourselves with what is being said.[37]

We next need to consider the topic of *private revelation*. At times, the New Testament speaks of the inner leading and witness of the Holy Spirit, such as when the Spirit prompts Philip to speak to the Ethiopian eunuch on the road to Gaza.[38] We have no good reason to think that this type of communication was limited to the days of the New Testament, so we should expect to receive private revelations or impressions from time to time.

The question that requires a considerable amount of attention is: Is there a way to determine with certainty that the message has come from the Holy Spirit? We sometimes assume that if a message sounds "spiritual," then it must be from God, but this is not the case. In his first letter, John tells us, "Beloved, do not believe every spirit, but test the spirits to see whether they are from God; for many false prophets have gone out into the world."[39] It is entirely possible to receive a spiritual message that does not come from the Holy Spirit. Therefore, there must be an appropriate "testing" of the message.

If we think the Spirit is communicating something to us, we should first turn to the Scriptures. As we have seen, the Spirit guided the human authors of the Bible like the wind moves a sailboat. He will not convey a message to us that ignores or contradicts anything he himself led the biblical writers to record. The Spirit is not schizophrenic. Thus, we can say that a person cannot possibly know if it is indeed the *Holy Spirit* speaking to him if he does not devote himself to the study of *Holy Scripture*. Beyond this, we can seek the counsel of those we know and trust, but even the godliest man or woman is not an infallible interpreter. At some point, we simply have to respond to the revelation and see what happens. If you think God is telling you to start your own business, then begin taking steps in that direction. If in time the business fails, you may have to admit that you were wrong about the source of the thought, or that God wanted you to fail so that you would learn to depend more on him and less on your own efforts. If the business succeeds, perhaps it was a genuine word from the Spirit, but it would be wrong for you to declare this to be the will of God for the entire church. Maybe God wanted you to start your own business, but he certainly does not want all believers to do this. The reason we know this is because it is not taught in Scripture, which is our common guide to God's will.[40] The written Word is "the only authority to which the church is called to submit *without reservation*."[41] We open the Scriptures with absolute certainty that these words come from God. In the church where I serve as pastor, when we read Scripture publicly—whether we read from Leviticus, Psalms, Matthew, or Romans—the reader concludes by saying, "*This is the Word of the Lord*," and the congregation responds, "Thanks be to God." When it comes to private revelations, we can never have this level of certainty. This is precisely why John tells us to "test the spirits."

Time for another brief warning. In certain circles, a great emphasis is placed upon private revelations and other special manifestations of the Spirit. It's as if those who experience such things have made it to the next level of Christianity; they've moved from the Minor to the Major League. My question is this: Why is it that we think we need more than the gospel? Why is it that the idea of some mystical experience or "fresh word from the Lord" is more exciting than the simple yet profound truth of Jesus Christ? When Karl Barth was asked about special manifestations, such as speaking in tongues, healing of sicknesses, and private revelations, he said, "Let us gather around the substance of the Gospel, around the Cross and the Resurrection! Here is our bread. And so long as we need bread we may not call out for cake!"[42] I'm with Barth on this one.

We move now to the Spirit's part in *sanctification*. The word "sanctification" refers to our growth in holiness. In some ways, spiritual growth is the opposite of physical growth. A mother or father holds a child's hand until the child learns to walk on his own. Spiritually speaking, we begin walking on our own, "following the course of this world, following the ruler of the power of the air, the spirit that is now at work among those who are disobedient."[43] Then the Holy Spirit regenerates us, brings us to Christ, and we learn to lean on Christ every step we take. A book on sanctification would never be found in the self-help section of Barnes and Noble (where all the kale-promoting books are), because sanctification is not about improving on our own. It's about depending on the resources of Christ, which are available to us because of the Holy Spirit. J. I. Packer says that Christian holiness is "consecrated closeness to God."[44] It is in essence worshiping God, obeying God, living for God, imitating God, taking God's side against sin, performing works that are pleasing to God, and loving God and others. All of this requires effort, so we shouldn't think of ourselves as remaining passive in the pursuit of holiness. But we certainly cannot do these things on our own, so we shouldn't think of sanctification as a solo mission. Sanctification requires *Spirit-empowered human effort.* Or as Paul puts it, *"Work out* your own salvation with fear and trembling; *for it is God who is at work in you,* enabling you both to will and to work for his good pleasure."[45]

The "work out" part means that we need to cultivate habits of holiness, such as Bible study and prayer, and as parents we need to cultivate these habits in front of our children.[46] Our children learn the importance of Bible study by watching us open the Bible day after day, and they learn how to pray by listening to us pray. Most nights I tuck my boys in and pray over them. I've done this since before they could talk. One of the things I pray over them often is a paraphrase of 3 John 4: "Lord, I pray that my boys would walk in the truth all the days of their lives." Not long after my younger son learned to talk, he told me that he wanted to say the nighttime prayer. After thanking God for his newest action figures and for the good pizza we had for dinner, Cullen said, "And God, I pray that my daddy would walk in the truth all the days of his life." It was at that moment that I got a little dust in my eye.

Finally, we come to the role of the Spirit in *service and mission*. As we think about service, we need to distinguish the *fruit* of the Spirit from the *gifts* of the Spirit. Love, joy, peace, patience, kindness, generosity, faithfulness, gentleness, and self-control: this is the *fruit* that all believers will display.[47] As all pear trees bear pears, so all those who have been inwardly transformed by the Spirit will bear the fruit of the Spirit. But when we think of the *gifts* of the Spirit, we need to picture a different type of tree—a Christmas tree.[48] Spiritual gifts are more like the gifts placed under the evergreen. They truly are gifts, distributed by the Spirit at his discretion. This means that we will have different gifts, but we should all have the same goal. Peter puts it like this: "Like good stewards of the manifold grace of God, serve one another with whatever gift each of you has received. Whoever speaks must do so as one speaking the very words of God; whoever serves must do so with the strength that God supplies, so that God may be glorified in all things through Jesus Christ."[49]

Every follower of Christ—even the tiniest one—has been gifted for ministry and sent out on mission. From the very beginning, the indwelling presence of the Holy Spirit has brought with it an evangelistic assignment: "You will receive power when the Holy Spirit has come upon you," Jesus said to his first disciples, "and you will be my witnesses in Jerusalem, in all Judea and Samaria, and to the ends of the earth."[50] Consistently, the Book of Acts presents those who are "filled with the Holy Spirit" as those who overflow with the message of Jesus.[51] The Holy Spirit causes us to become joyfully obsessed with the gospel message, and he empowers us to share this message with a profound boldness. But the New Testament is equally clear that this same Spirit must penetrate the heart of the hearer for the message to be truly received.[52] Christians have no concept of conversion by coercion. We cannot put a knife to a man's neck and make him become a genuine believer. Nor can we argue someone into the family of God by gentler means. All Christians are called to share the gospel with the people whom God sovereignly places in our paths, but the Holy Spirit is the great persuader. As Martin Luther once said, it's the Christian's task to get the gospel from his mouth to his neighbor's ear; it's the Holy Spirit's task to get the gospel from the ear to the heart.

SCRATCHING DRAGONS, TALKING TO STATUES

What this means is that, ultimately, the conversion of our children is out of our hands. Conversion is something *they cannot do for themselves*, and it is something *we cannot do for them*. Two scenes in C. S. Lewis's Narnia stories illustrate these truths particularly well. The first is found in *The Voyage of the Dawn Treader*. One of the main characters, a brat of a child named Eustace Clarence Scrubb, is transformed into a dragon. Hoping to escape from the terrifying form, Eustace begins scratching himself, and as he does, his scales and eventually his skin begin to peel off. But every time one layer of skin comes off, Eustace finds another layer beneath it. After a while of clawing away at himself, Eustace becomes frustrated, saying, "How ever many skins have I got to take off?"[53] At this moment the Great Lion, Aslan, says to Eustace, "You will have to let me undress you."[54]

Eustace is afraid of the Lion's claws, but beyond desperation, he lies down flat on his back, submitting himself to the Lion. Aslan's claws succeed where Eustace's had failed; the Lion cuts all the way to the heart. Only Aslan is able to "un-dragon" the beastly boy.[55]

The second scene is found near the end of *The Lion, the Witch and the Wardrobe*. After Aslan has been killed and raised from the dead, he takes Lucy and Susan to the White Witch's castle. With the two girls on his back, Aslan leaps over the castle wall and lands in the courtyard, which is full of statues. These statues once were living creatures of Narnia, but now they are under the White Witch's dark magic. Lucy and Susan are powerless in the courtyard. Lucy's dear friend, Mr. Tumnus, is frozen in stone, but there is nothing she can do to set him free. Nothing except call out to Aslan. Because Aslan can help him. Aslan can help them all. He approaches the statues, breathes on them, and one by one, the creatures of Narnia come to life.[56]

The Bible teaches us that true conversion is always a miracle; it is always the supernatural work of God. Take the power of God out of the equation and we're left to transform a dragon by scratching him or to bring a stone statue to life by talking to it. It'll never work. Of course, I'm not suggesting that parent-theologians are entirely passive, that there is no need for us to teach and model the gospel in our homes. Throughout this book, I've been making the opposite case! What I'm saying now is that the most important thing we must do is cry out to Aslan, cry out to God, asking him to do in our children what only he can do. Only he can cut to the heart. Only he can turn stone into flesh.

FAMILY WORSHIP GUIDE

The Apostles' Creed

As a family, memorize the fifth part of the Creed.

I believe in the Holy Spirit.

Key Verses

In addition to memorizing the fifth part of the Creed, choose one or more of the following passages to treasure in your heart:

THE FLOODLIGHT MINISTRY OF THE HOLY SPIRIT

When the Spirit of truth comes, he will guide you into all the truth, for he will not speak on his own authority, but whatever he hears he will speak, and he will declare to you the things that are to come. He will glorify me, for he will take what is mine and declare it to you. (John 16:13–14 NIV)

THE INDWELLING PRESENCE OF THE HOLY SPIRIT

And I will put my Spirit within you, and cause you to walk in my statutes and be careful to obey my rules. (Ezekiel 36:27 NIV)

THE GIVER OF SPIRITUAL LIFE

Jesus answered, "Truly, truly, I say to you, unless one is born of water and the Spirit, he cannot enter the kingdom of God." (John 3:5 NIV)

A NEW WAY OF LIFE

Therefore, if anyone is in Christ, he is a new creation. The old has passed away; behold, the new has come. (2 Corinthians 5:17 NIV)

THE HOLY SPIRIT AND SCRIPTURE

For no prophecy was ever produced by the will of man, but men spoke from God as they were carried along by the Holy Spirit. (2 Peter 1:21 NIV)

THE HOLY SPIRIT AND MISSION

But you will receive power when the Holy Spirit has come upon you, and you will be my witnesses in Jerusalem and in all Judea and Samaria, and to the end of the earth. (Acts 1:8 NIV)

Nuggets of Truth

Parent-theologians, when teaching your children-disciples, be sure to cover these main points from Chapter 5:

HE WHO IS GOD

- Christians affirm the *three-in-oneness* of God. Though there is only *one* true God, this God eternally exists as *three* distinct persons: Father, Son, and Holy Spirit. Each person is fully God.

- When we say that God eternally exists in three distinct *persons*, we do not mean that he exists as three *human beings* or that he has *three bodies*. Only Jesus, the God-*man*, has a body.

- By *person*, we mean that the Spirit is not a force, a cloud, or a vapor. The Spirit is not an *it*; the Spirit is a *he*. Like the Father and the Son, he is able to give and receive love.

- As the third person of the Trinity, the Spirit has always existed and has always been at work in the world.

- But the Spirit comes *in a new way* in Acts 2. On the Day of Pentecost, the Spirit comes to indwell believers, making a permanent home in their hearts.

HE WHO GIVES LIFE

- As descendants of Adam, all human beings are sinful or corrupt to the very core of our being. Another way to put this is to say, as Paul does in Ephesians 2:1, that we are *spiritually dead*.

- The Holy Spirit breathes new life into our spiritual corpses. In theological terms, this is the sovereign and gracious work of *regeneration*.

- When the Spirit brings us to life (regeneration), he reveals to our minds and seals upon our hearts the truth of God's love for us (faith), and the result is that we forsake our sin and follow Jesus as Lord (repentance).

- Our born-again identity will become increasingly evident in our conversations and conduct. The same will be true of our children. What we're looking for in our children is *progressive sanctification* (growth in holiness), not *sinless perfection*.

- If we see in our children a consistent struggle against sin, submission to God's authority, and love for God and others, then we can be certain that God has done a gracious and mighty work in them, and that they have eternal fellowship with him.

HE WHO GUIDES AND EMPOWERS

- The Holy Spirit is the revealer, teacher, and persuader who guides us to an understanding of Christ's teaching, and he is the empowering presence who enables us to do the work of Christ in the world.

- *Inspiration.* The Spirit guided the Old Testament and the New Testament writers in such a way that with their human hands they wrote the very message of God.

- *Illumination.* It is the inward work of the Spirit that enables us to welcome the Word of God, seeing the message as true and aligning ourselves with what is being said.

- *Private Revelation.* The Bible speaks of the inner leading and witness of the Spirit. When we think the Spirit is speaking to us, there must be an appropriate "testing" of the message (1 John 4:1).

- *Sanctification.* The word "sanctification" refers to growth in holiness, which happens through Spirit-empowered human effort. We need to cultivate habits of holiness, such as Bible study and prayer, and as parents, we need to cultivate these habits in front of our children.

- *Service and Mission.* Every follower of Christ—even the tiniest one—has been gifted for ministry and sent out on mission. The Spirit causes us to become joyfully obsessed with the gospel, and he empowers us to serve others and share Christ's message with a profound boldness.

Questions for the Family

Use these questions to spark discussion during your family worship times:

HE WHO IS GOD

- What do we mean when we say that the Holy Spirit is a person?

- How has the Holy Spirit shown his love for us?

- What happens in Acts 2? How is the Spirit's presence with us now different from his presence with believers prior to Acts 2?

HE WHO GIVES LIFE

- In John 3:5, Jesus says that we must be "born of the Spirit." What does this mean?

- What is faith?

- What is repentance?

- Can we know that we have eternal fellowship (a forever relationship) with God? If so, how do we know? What are the evidences or signs of this fellowship?

HE WHO GUIDES AND EMPOWERS

- What part did the Holy Spirit play in the writing of the Bible? How important is the Bible in the Christian life?

- What should we do if we think the Spirit is speaking to us?

- How is the Spirit working in your life currently, making you more like Jesus? In what areas do you need to grow?

- Do we have any family members or friends who don't know Jesus? How can we share his love with them?

Songs That Celebrate These Truths

As you study the truths summarized in part five of the Creed, also celebrate these truths as a family. Sing the following songs together, and try to memorize at least the first verse of each one.

- "More About Jesus Would I Know"

- "Breathe on Me, Breath of God"

Prayer Prompts

Always conclude your family worship times with prayer. Here are some prayer themes to keep in mind while your family studies this part of the Creed:

- Thankfulness for the Holy Spirit's work in us, bringing spiritual life and providing the gift of faith

- Our struggle against sin and ongoing growth in holiness

- Greater appreciation and understanding of God's Word

- Faithful participation in God's worldwide mission

6
The Church

I believe in ... the holy catholic church,
the communion of saints,
the forgiveness of sins ...

WHY WE CAN'T BE "DONE" WITH THE CHURCH

At the outset of this book, I called you to think of yourself as
a parent-theologian, as the one primarily responsible for opening up the Scriptures to help your children understand God, the
world, and themselves. But I also insisted that participation in
a Christ-exalting local church is crucial. To put it bluntly: *You*
and your children need the fellowship of believers.

My parents are committed Christ-followers, and they
raised their three boys on a healthy diet of God's Word and in
the context of the local church. My dad was the spiritual leader
of our home. He led imperfectly, as we all do, but he consistently pointed us to Christ, and he made it clear that for the

Thornton household, church attendance and participation were mandatory. In my preteen years my enthusiasm for church dwindled, or maybe it was just that my zeal for sleeping late and being lazy escalated. Occasionally, I would try to get out of attending church with my family: "Dad, I don't think I can go to church today. I feel really sick." My dad's response was simple: "Sick, huh? Throw up and prove it." If I couldn't throw up, we went to church. And if I could throw up, Dad would just smile and say, "Well, I bet you feel better now. Let's go to church."

Underlying my dad's insistence was the conviction that the Christian life is *life in community*, or as Dietrich Bonhoeffer puts it, *life together*. In his classic work on Christian community, Bonhoeffer claims, "The physical presence of other Christians is a source of incomparable joy and strength to the believer."[1] But these words were published in 1954, in a world where "physical presence" was virtually the only presence. By and large, people don't value life-on-life relationships, face-to-face conversations as they once did; instead, we prefer digital interaction, an editable self, delete-able friends.[2] For decades, sociologists have been telling us about the increasing number of people who appear to be developing a severe allergy to organized community. Most disconcerting is the research indicating that scores of Christians claim that the church in particular is unnecessary. Some even go so far as to assert that the church is a hindrance to their relationship with God. Sociologist Josh Packard documents the anti-church mind-set in his recent work, *Church Refugees*. Packard's book is about "people who make an explicit and intentional decision to leave the church."[3] He refers to these individuals as "the dechurched" or "the Dones"; they're people who, for various reasons, are done with church, fed up with organized fellowship, convinced that the Christian life is best lived apart from the institutional church. I realize that today the trendy thing to do is "jump church," but for the spiritual health of your family, I implore you to follow the lead of the octogenarian who wears white knee-high socks with his sandals: be blatantly unfashionable.

Remember that the Apostles' Creed states the core truths of the Christian faith. According to the Creed, the doctrine of the church is an essential matter. The church is not an add-on, like bacon for your burger. Though I suppose if the church were like bacon, then everyone would love the church. As the wise man once said, "Either you like bacon or you're wrong." No local church is perfect, so every church will at some point let you down. But the faults of local fellowships do not provide an excuse to give up on the church as a whole. Honestly, the Dones haven't really thought the matter through. An anti-church Christ-follower is a contradiction in terms if ever there was one. You can't say, "Jesus, yes; church, no," because Jesus himself says, "Church, yes."[4] In point of fact, the church is Christ's masterpiece, created by his blood for the purpose of displaying his glory to the world.

FOUR ESSENTIAL FEATURES OF THE PEOPLE OF GOD

The Creed concludes with these words: "I believe in...the holy catholic church, the communion of saints, the forgiveness of sins, the resurrection of the body, and the life everlasting. Amen." Previously, we learned that forgiveness of sin is found in Jesus Christ alone, and that all those who place their faith in Christ have the hope of bodily resurrection and eternal life in the new creation. In this final chapter, we'll center our discussion on "the holy catholic church, the communion of saints." Notice, first of all, that the Creed speaks of "*the* church." In the New Testament, the word translated as "church" is the word *ekklē-sia*, which means "assembly" or "community." When we hear the word "church" today, we probably think of a *place* where people gather. Perhaps we picture a great cathedral, like Notre Dame or Westminster Abbey. Or maybe we think of something simpler, like a red brick building with a white steeple. A certain stream within contemporary Christianity tends to criticize buildings. But buildings in themselves are not bad things. Gathering with other believers in a designated space for the purpose of worshiping God has always been a central Christian practice. It's important, however, to understand that the word "church" does not refer to property or structures, but to *people*, peculiar people.

What are the essential features of this peculiar people? Historically, four features have been identified. Three of these are mentioned in the Apostles' Creed. All four appear in the Nicene-Constantinopolitan Creed: "We believe in one, holy, catholic, and apostolic Church." We could also put it this way: the people of God are known for their *unity, purity, inclusivity,* and *exclusivity.*

First, the people of God are known for their *unity.* To understand the unity or oneness of the church, we must return (again) to the doctrine of the triunity of God. The one true God eternally exists in three distinct persons. Among the persons of the Trinity there has always been a perfect communion, a holy unity. The church participates in this unity; we have entered into fellowship with the Father by union with the Son through the power of the Holy Spirit.[5] The *"one* Spirit" unites us to the "*one* Lord," and he unites us to one another, making us the "*one* body" of Christ.[6] In the preceding chapter, we looked at how the Spirit came in a new way on the Day of Pentecost. Pentecost was the beautiful reversal of the Tower of Babel.[7] At the beginning of Genesis 11, the whole earth had one language. The people were unified, but they were unified in their pursuit of self-glory; they wanted to make a name for themselves.[8] Babel was an act of division and confusion because of this self-glorification. At Pentecost, the Spirit descends, binding believers together in one community that is devoted to the glory of God, set on seeking the fame of the name "Jesus Christ."[9]

Unity is a theological reality, something *God has created for us*. But unity is also something *the church must maintain*. In Ephesians 4:3, Paul calls us to "make every effort to maintain the unity of the Spirit in the bond of peace." Members of the one body must grow in our apprehension and demonstration of unity, better understanding and more clearly expressing this God-given truth. For the people of God to live in disunity is to live in disagreement with our true identity. We *are* the one body of Christ. To act otherwise is to act *against* the reconciling work of our Savior and Lord.[10]

Second, the people of God are people of *purity*. The Apostles' Creed speaks of "the *holy* church" and "the communion of *saints*." Like the word "church," the term "holy" is frequently misunderstood. Many Christians hear the word "holiness" and picture something like a ladder leading up to heaven. Each rung on the ladder is a command, and every obedient step brings us closer and closer to God, thus making us holier and holier. If we get high enough, we might even begin to glow. The problem with this way of thinking is that it fails to realize that holiness is something the church already possesses. Holiness, like unity, is a theological reality, something God has provided for us, not something we must strive to attain on our own. The church is holy because it has been drawn into the holiness of God himself, into the fellowship of the Holy Trinity. Throughout the Bible, people, places, and even things are referred to as holy because of their association with God. In Exodus 3, Moses is keeping the flock of his father-in-law when suddenly a bush catches fire. This is Katniss Everdeen fire; the bush is blazing, but it's not being consumed. Out of this unconsumed shrubbery comes the voice of God, "Come no closer! Remove the sandals from your feet, for the place on which you are standing is holy ground."[11] Why is the ground holy? Because God is there! The dirt *is* holy because of the divine presence. In like manner, the church *is* holy because we have been drawn into fellowship with the Father by union with the Son through the power of the Holy Spirit.

The church is holy in a once and for all sense. Holiness, like unity, is a theological reality. But here again Scripture teaches us that we must grow in our apprehension and demonstration of this reality. According to John 17, we have been called "out of the world" and sent back "into the world," where we bear witness to the truth without being "of the world." Or as James puts it, we must keep ourselves "unstained from the world."[12] James is calling us to choose purity over popularity. The late Calvin Miller was a good friend and ministry mentor of mine. He was a well-known pastor and author. In one of his sermons, Calvin told the story of a trip he once took to Pisa, Italy. Of course, while in Pisa he went to see the infamous Leaning Tower. Calvin climbed the great cathedral tower, slanted some thirteen feet off perpendicular at the time of his visit. He described the feeling of uneasiness that came over him as he ascended what seemed an unstable structure. When he arrived safely on solid ground, he turned to the tour guide and asked, "Sir, will this tower destroy itself one day?" "Yes, I suppose it will," the tour guide said. Calvin replied, "Is there anything you can do to save it?" "Sure," the guide said. "Lots of things. Why, we could probably even straighten it." Perplexed by the guide's response, Calvin asked, "Well, if you can save it, why don't you?" "Let me ask you a question," the guide said. "Would you have come to Pisa today if our bell tower had been straight?" Then he said, "We care far more about being popular than we do about being straight."

The illustration requires little comment. Suffice it to say that all Christians walk in the context of an unholy world, a place where sinful practices are popular. The businesswoman is often under tremendous pressure to compromise ethical and legal standards in order to satisfy the greed of her superiors. The university student finds himself in an environment drenched with alcohol and polluted with lust. Even our youngest children will have many peers who do not share our Christian values.[13] As I've said before, holiness does not mean sinlessness. The church on earth is the community of the forgiven, the faithful, but not the flawless. Without expecting our children to be perfect, from their earliest years we should teach them to pursue purity and holiness. We should raise our children to know that our family is different—without apologizing for it! Habitually,

I say to my sons, "Boys, remember that wherever you go, you are three things: a Christian, a Thornton, and a gentleman." The latter two are important, but the primary point I want them to remember is their identity in Christ and their responsibility to live as Christ's people in the world. They, along with all believers, are "a chosen race, a royal priesthood, a holy nation, God's own people," and their ultimate purpose in this life is to proclaim both in word and deed "the mighty acts of him who called [them] out of darkness into his marvelous light."[14]

Finally, the people of God are known for both *inclusivity* and *exclusivity*. This is my gloss on the third and fourth historical attributes of the church: catholicity and apostolicity. When the Apostles' Creed speaks of "the *catholic* church" it doesn't mean "Roman Catholic." Rather, it means "universal." The church is not restricted by geography, ethnicity, socioeconomic class, age, gender, hair color, or personality type. By his blood, Christ ransomed saints from "every tribe and language and people and nation."[15] The catholicity of the church means that we are an *inclusive* community: "*Everyone* who calls on the name of the Lord shall be saved."[16]

Additionally, the church is "apostolic" because it is founded on the teaching of the apostles, the center of which is Jesus Christ, and also because of its charge to carry out the

Great Commission.[17] The apostolic gospel is a deposit of truth, but not a deposit to be sealed up for safekeeping. It is, rather, the worldwide word of salvation, the one message all people desperately need to hear: people in North America, Asia, Australia, and across the globe. The apostolicity of the church means that we are an *exclusive* community: "Everyone *who calls on the name of the Lord* shall be saved." In an effort to make the message of the church more suitable for the modern ear, some groups have sought to upgrade the gospel, eliminating all offensive elements, suggesting that Christ is simply one of many life-giving choices on the spiritual buffet. Such groups cannot be considered part of the true church, because they deny the reality of the one timeless and universal message of salvation: Christ died for our sins, he was buried, and he was raised on the third day in accordance with the Scriptures.[18] The core message of the true church will always be that the person and work of Jesus Christ is the one hope for sinners. New Testament scholar Michael Bird's comment is apropos: "What the church has to offer the world is not our architecture, our programs, our press releases, our politics, our clergy, or even our potlucks. The best thing and really the only thing we have to offer is Jesus Christ. The one thing that the church can offer that no other organization or institution can is Jesus as Lord and Savior of all peoples. The mission of this peculiar people called the church is to live and love, serve and sing, preach and teach that Jesus Christ is Lord."[19]

THREE QUESTIONS TO ASK OF A POTENTIAL CHURCH HOME

The *universal church* is the company of Christ-followers stretching from the Day of Pentecost to the return of Christ, including both believers who are presently in heaven and living believers from all over the world. The universal church finds expression in *local fellowships*.[20] First Baptist, Second Presbyterian, Christ the King Anglican, Owaka Grace Fellowship, Faith Community Church: these are examples of local fellowships. Let's say you and your family have been disconnected from a local church for a while, or maybe you've recently transitioned to a new area and soon will be searching for a new church home. What should be your top criteria as you search? A certain style of music? Stadium seating in the worship room? Cutting-edge technology? A fancy bookstore that serves complicated coffee drinks? An exciting children's area complete with a three-story slide? While adults like their coffee and kids love their slides, none of these things help us identify a true and healthy local church, and this should be our primary concern.

Responsible parents will have a list of more serious matters to investigate: Is the children's wing secure? Does this church have a child protection policy? What curriculum is being used in the children's ministry? Is the primary goal to entertain my children or to help disciple them?

But three key questions should rise to the top of the list:[21]

The first question parents should ask of a potential church home: *Does this congregation prioritize the preaching and teaching of God's Word, and especially the gospel?*

Local churches are led by divinely called and biblically qualified individuals usually referred to as "pastors" or "elders," shepherd-leaders who have the responsibility of feeding, leading, protecting, and caring for the portion of the Lord's flock entrusted to them.[22] Just as the primary task of the parent is to serve God's Word in the home, the primary task of the pastor is to serve the Word in the household of God. "Preach the word," Paul said to Timothy. "Be ready in season and out of season; reprove, rebuke, and exhort, with complete patience and teaching. For the time is coming when people will not endure sound teaching, but having itching ears they will accumulate for themselves teachers to suit their own passions."[23] I fear the time of which Paul spoke has arrived. Preaching is less popular now than ever before. The Lord's Day proclamation of the Word is being replaced with dramatic storytelling, video clips, and casual conversations. Not long ago I attended a "worship service" where a team of people with highlighted hair, stylish clothes, and caffeinated beverages (swiped from the on-site bookstore, no doubt) walked onstage, each one pulled up a bar-stool, and they proceeded to have a seven-minute conversation about something culturally relevant, with the occasional sprin-kle of Bible to bring a bit of godly flavor to the discussion—but not too much! Other congregations have retained the idea of the preacher, but the sermon(ettes) are biblically and theologically anemic: "Twelve Steps to Your Best Life Now" or "Eight Unde-niable Qualities of a Winner." The children of God—from the youngest to the oldest—need the Word of God, not platitudes, anecdotes, or opinion pieces. Nothing is more important than finding a local fellowship where the pastor walks the people through the Scriptures, book-by-book, chapter-by-chapter, verse-by-verse, a place where the whole counsel of God is pro-claimed faithfully, clearly, and passionately, where the gospel is heralded again, and again, and again.

With all this talk about preaching and worship services, I imagine some of you are wondering: Is it better for children to remain in corporate worship, "big church," or to be dismissed from their parents for a time of age-appropriate teaching, "children's church"? Certainly, all children need age-appropriate instruction, both in the home and in the household of God, but my contention is that the latter is best achieved through the avenues of Sunday school, Awana, or something similar. I suggest that, from first grade (or so) up, children should participate in corporate worship with their parents.[24] I say this for one primary reason. Recall the fundamental presupposition of this book: Christian parents are responsible for the spiritual development of the children under their care. Why, then, would we gather our families for Lord's Day worship only to send our children off to learn from someone else? This is not at all to call into question the role of children's directors or Sunday school teachers. As I've said, these faithful servants have a formative function in the church. But during corporate worship, children should learn from their parents. They should sit with us, observing how we bow our heads in prayer, how we sing praises to God with joy on our faces, and how we listen eagerly to the preaching of God's Word. Parents should model for their children white-hot worship of the almighty God. Here I suspect that John and Noel Piper are right when they conclude, "The greatest stumbling block for children in worship is that their parents do not cherish the hour. Children can feel the difference between duty and delight. Therefore, the first and most important job of a parent is to fall in love with the worship of God. You can't impart what you don't possess."[25]

Over the years I've encountered a number of objections to the proposal that children should remain in corporate worship. The most common one goes something like this: "It's unreasonable to expect a young child to sit quietly for an hour." I usually respond to this one with the utmost pastoral sensitivity: Bull. Turn on their favorite cartoon on Netflix and my boys will sit quietly until Jesus comes back. I bet your children are the same way. They're capable of being still, and they can learn to do so in the context of corporate worship. Parents who feel helpless to control their rambunctious children should seek to solve the dilemma not by sending the wild ones off to an alternative service, but by renewing discipline in the home. "Children, obey your parents in the Lord, for this is right," Paul says.[26] And this includes when they say, "Sit still, and pay attention." Implementing or revitalizing the practice of family worship, as I hope this book will help you do, will go a long way in helping make your children ready for corporate worship. "The very earliest 'school' for worship is in the home."[27]

Another objection I often hear is, " 'Big church' is over their heads." No, it isn't. Children absorb far more than we/they realize, and this is true even when they say they are bored. As we sing great hymns of the faith, our children are infused with a deep sense of the majesty of God. At least a few times a week my boys wake up singing "Holy, Holy, Holy." By far, these are my favorite moments of the week. Even if parts of the pastor's sermon go over the heads of the little ones, my years in ministry have taught me that children are better than we think at catching the big truths of the Bible. And unquestionably what they will catch is that there is something special about gathering with God's people, with Mom and Dad, around *this Book*. Moreover, if parents will encourage their child to "listen with claws," to seize the words of the sermon, and then ask questions on the ride home or over lunch about what he or she learned that day, the child's capacity to comprehend the message and participate in all aspects of worship will increase dramatically.

The second question parents should ask: *Is this a place that prioritizes the sacraments of baptism and communion?*

Some denominations prefer to call baptism and communion (or the Lord's Supper) "ordinances"; these are celebrations "ordained" by Christ himself. At the end of Matthew's Gospel, Jesus says, "All authority in heaven and on earth has been given to me. Go therefore and make disciples of all nations, baptizing them in the name of the Father and of the Son and of the Holy Spirit."[28] Christ also commands his people to gather around his table. In 1 Corinthians 11:23–26, Paul writes, "For I received from the Lord what I also handed on to you, that the Lord Jesus on the night when he was betrayed took a loaf of bread, and when he had given thanks, he broke it and said, 'This is my body that is for you. Do this in remembrance of me.' In the same way he took the cup also, after supper, saying, 'This cup is the new covenant in my blood. Do this, as often as you drink it, in remembrance of me.' For as often as you eat this bread and drink the cup, you proclaim the Lord's death until he comes." The sacraments are God-given art, the visual aids that complement the preaching of the Word. We *see* the gospel every time we baptize someone or gather around the communion table.

While denominations differ on the details—*how* and *when* a person should be baptized and *what* exactly is taking place at the communion table—it is important for parents to realize that every true and healthy local church will practice the sacraments. Because Christ himself has expressly commanded these ceremonies, there can be no truly Christian church without them. This means that there is a lengthy list of gatherings that, though helpful, do not constitute a local church. When I was working on my PhD in Dunedin, New Zealand, I gathered regularly at a local pub with several other biblical studies and theology students. We had a few pints, talked about Didymus the Blind, John Calvin, Karl Barth, and a bunch of other dead guys, and sometimes even inquired about personal and family matters. I greatly enjoyed these pub chats, but it would have been foolish for me to maintain that these gatherings were all I needed, that this was my "church." Sadly, I've heard many Christians claim that they have church with a few hunting pals in the woods, or with fishing buddies on their boat, or even while walking solitarily along the beach. Such times with the Lord can be calming, encouraging, and spiritually beneficial for us, but they are not church. The true church is marked by the proclamation of the Bible and the demonstration of the gospel in the practices of baptism and communion. As one of the dead guys frequently discussed in my old pub chats says, "Wherever we see the Word of God purely preached and heard, and the sacraments administered according to Christ's institution, there, it is not to be doubted, a church of God exists."[29]

The third question parents should ask when visiting a potential church home: *Does this congregation regularly exercise church discipline?*

Understood rightly, church discipline is an act, not of domination, but of devotion. A true Christian community is a place where mutual affection leads to mutual accountability.[30] The earliest Christians were known as "followers of the Way."[31] They believed that the Way led somewhere and that those who strayed from the Way needed to be brought back to it. In metaphorical terms, the church is composed of people willing to serve as both guides and search and rescue operators. A few summers ago I decided to climb Long's Peak, one of Colorado's best-known 14ers. The Keyhole route is roughly 15 miles round trip, with over 5,000 feet of elevation gain, climaxing with a glorious view from 14,255 feet. It's a stunning but perilous trek. Dozens and dozens of people have died trying to summit Long's. Fortunately, I made it to the top without a scratch, but not because I'm an expert climber. Far from it. I reached the summit because I decided not to hike alone. I tackled Long's with my buddy, Zach, a far more experienced climber who had summited Long's several times before. He had seen things I hadn't seen, been places I hadn't been. He could lead the way, glance back at me occasionally, and say, "Come this way; *don't* go that way." Similarly, we need the guidance of other believers to help us remain on the (up)right path. And when we stray toward danger—as we all do at times—we need brothers and sisters in Christ who love us enough to come after us. When considering a local fellowship, we should ask: Will these fellow travelers love my children and me enough to hold us account-able, to admonish us when we go astray? Bonhoeffer puts it beautifully: "Nothing can be more cruel than the tenderness that consigns another to his sin. Nothing can be more compas-sionate than the severe rebuke that calls a brother back from the path of sin."[32]

In sum, your family needs a church home, a genuine and vigorous fellowship where you will *hear* the gospel (preach-ing/teaching), *see* the gospel (the sacraments), and find the help you need to *display* the gospel in your daily lives (disci-pline). You need brothers and sisters in Christ who will come alongside you as parent-theologians in your task of making children-disciples.

CONCLUDING AND BEGINNING AGAIN: WE NEVER OUTGROW OUR NEED FOR THE GOSPEL

Having come to the end of the Apostles' Creed and thus to the end of our study, the obvious question is: Where do we go from here? What should we do when we have finished reading this book, finished working our way through the Family Worship Guides? That's an easy one: Keep reciting and unpacking the Creed as a family. And gather additional resources that will help you and your children grow in your understanding of the gospel. The gospel is not grade-school theology that we replace with higher-level content as we grow. The gospel is not like training wheels on a bike; it's not something we start with but eventually can make do without. We never outgrow our need for the gospel.

In his biography *The Wright Brothers* David McCullough tells the story of Wilbur and Orville, two Ohio boys who, with no college education, no formal technical training, and very little money, set out on a mission to fly.[33] In August 1900, the brothers built a glider large enough to carry a man. The wingspan was eighteen feet. The total cost of the glider was $15. On December 17, 1903, for the very first time, Orville flew the Wright brothers' flying machine. "Were you scared?" Orville would be asked. "Scared?" he said with a smile. "There wasn't time for that." The total distance flown had been only 120 feet. The first flight had lasted only twelve seconds. On August 8, 1908, Wilbur showed the world what the Wright's invention could do. It was the first public demonstration of their flying machine, and within twenty-four hours it was headline news everywhere. As one source put it, "It was not merely a success, but a triumph...a decisive victory for aviation." Here's the most fascinating piece of the story. Long before the Wright brothers conquered the air, long before their flying machine was built, Wilbur would sit for hours at a time studying the birds, noticing their every movement, filling his journal with notes. This great victory for aviation started with something so simple: Wilbur Wright looking again and again at the birds.

If your children are like mine, they want to hear the same stories over and over again. "Dad, tell me about the time you dialed 911 as a child and the firemen came to your house thinking it was a real emergency." "But boys, you've heard that story a million times." "We don't care. We want to hear it again!" There's one story we want our children to fall in love with more than any other: the story summarized in the Apostles' Creed, the great gospel story. And as we tell this simple yet profound story, great things will happen; our children will find their places in the story. They will come to see that they are children of the Father, reconciled by the blood of the Son, regenerated by the Holy Spirit, members of the one body, created for the ultimate purpose of displaying God's glory to the world. So, parents, tell your daughter the gospel story—from the time you bring her home from the hospital. Tell your son the gospel story—until the day he drives away on his honeymoon. Never stop telling this story. Give your children Jesus. Again. And again. And again.

FAMILY WORSHIP GUIDE

The Apostles' Creed

As a family, memorize the final part of the Creed in three simple steps.

> *I believe in the Holy Spirit, the holy catholic church,*
>> *the communion of saints,*
> *the forgiveness of sins, the resurrection of the body,*
> *and the life everlasting. Amen.*

Key Verses

In addition to memorizing the final part of the Creed, choose one or more of the following passages to treasure in your heart:

THE UNITY OF THE CHURCH

> *Make every effort to keep the unity of the Spirit through the bond of peace. There is one body and one Spirit, just as you were called to one hope when you were called; one Lord, one faith, one baptism; one God and Father of all, who is over all and through all and in all. (Ephesians 4:3–6 NIV)*

THE PURITY OF THE CHURCH

But you are a chosen people, a royal priesthood, a holy nation, God's special possession, that you may declare the praises of him who called you out of darkness into his wonderful light. (1 Peter 2:9 NIV)

THE INCLUSIVITY AND EXCLUSIVITY OF THE CHURCH

As Scripture says, "Anyone who believes in him will never be put to shame." For there is no difference between Jew and Gentile—the same Lord is Lord of all and richly blesses all who call on him, for, "Everyone who calls on the name of the Lord will be saved." (Romans 10:11–13 NIV)

THE MISSION OF THE CHURCH

Then Jesus came to them and said, "All authority in heaven and on earth has been given to me. Therefore go and make disciples of all nations, baptizing them in the name of the Father and of the Son and of the Holy Spirit, and teaching them to obey everything I have commanded you. And surely I am with you always, to the very end of the age." (Matthew 28:18–20 NIV)

Nuggets of Truth

Parent-theologians, when teaching your children-disciples, be sure to cover these main points from Chapter 6:

FOUR ESSENTIAL FEATURES OF THE PEOPLE OF GOD

- When we hear the word "church" today, we probably think of a *place*; however, it's important to remember that, biblically speaking, the term "church" refers, not to property or structures, but to *people*.

- The people of God are known for their *unity*, *purity*, *inclusivity*, and *exclusivity*.

  ° Unity: The "one Spirit" unites us to the "one Lord," and he unites us to one another, making us the "one body" of Christ.

  ° Purity or Holiness: The church is holy because it has been drawn into the holiness of God himself, into the fellowship of the Holy Trinity.

  ° Inclusivity or Catholicity: The church is not restricted by geography, ethnicity, socioeconomic class, age, gender, hair color, or personality type. By his blood, Christ ransomed saints from "every tribe and language and people and nation" (Revelation 5:9).

○ Exclusivity or Apostolicity: The apostolic gospel is
a deposit of truth, but not a deposit to be sealed up
for safekeeping. It is, rather, the worldwide word of
salvation, the one message all people desperately need
to hear. The core message of the true church will always
be that the person and work of Jesus Christ is the one
hope for sinners.

THREE QUESTIONS TO ASK OF A POTENTIAL CHURCH HOME

- The *universal church* is the company of Christ-followers
stretching from the Day of Pentecost to the return of
Christ, including both believers who are presently in
heaven and living believers from all over the world. The
universal church finds expression in *local fellowships*.

- When searching for a local fellowship, a church home, we
should look for three things in particular: *the preaching of
God's Word, the administration of the sacraments, and the
exercise of church discipline*.

- The preaching and teaching of God's Word, and especially
the gospel: Nothing is more important than finding
a local fellowship where the pastor walks the people
through the Scriptures, book-by-book, chapter-by-chapter,
verse-by-verse, a place where the whole counsel of God is

proclaimed faithfully, clearly, and passionately, where the gospel is heralded again, and again, and again.

- The administration of baptism and communion: The sacraments are God-given art, the visual aids that complement the preaching of the Word. We *see* the gospel every time we baptize someone or gather around the communion table.

- The exercise of church discipline: A true Christian community is a place where mutual affection leads to mutual accountability. We need the guidance of other believers to help us remain on the upright path. And when we stray toward danger—as we all do at times—we need brothers and sisters in Christ who love us enough to come after us.

- In sum, your family needs a church home, a genuine and vigorous fellowship where you will *hear* the gospel (preaching/teaching), *see* the gospel (the sacraments), and find the help you need to *display* the gospel in your daily lives (discipline).

Questions for the Family

Use these questions to spark discussion during your family worship times:

FOUR ESSENTIAL FEATURES OF THE PEOPLE OF GOD

- What does the word "church" mean?

- What does it mean to display the unity God has created for us? Or to state the question differently: How do we live peaceably (live without arguing or fighting) with other members of the church?

- The Bible teaches us that we must keep ourselves "unstained from the world" (James 1:27). What does this mean? How can we keep ourselves pure for God?

- Why is it so important to share the message of Jesus with everyone?

THREE QUESTIONS TO ASK OF A POTENTIAL CHURCH HOME

- What are the three most important things to look for in a local fellowship, a church home?

- Why is the preaching of God's Word so important?

- How do baptism and communion teach us about the gospel?

- What is church discipline? How can we encourage each other and help each other stay on the path of godliness?

Songs That Celebrate These Truths

As you study the truths summarized in part six of the Creed, also celebrate these truths as a family. Sing the following songs together, and try to memorize at least the first verse of each one.

- "The Church's One Foundation"

- "I Love to Tell the Story"

Prayer Prompts

Always conclude your family worship times with prayer. Here are some prayer themes to keep in mind while your family studies this final part of the Creed:

- Maintaining the unity God has created; living peaceably with our brothers and sisters in Christ

- Pursuing purity as God's special people in a sinful world

- Boldness to share the message of Jesus with everyone God places in our family's path

- Local fellowships throughout the world, that they would remain gospel-centered in their ministries

Acknowledgments

I wish to thank Larry and Pam Thornton, my parents, who have lovingly and consistently pointed me to Jesus for over three decades; Scott Stevenson, my youth pastor who made a tremendous impact on me when I was very young; Ric Callahan, my first ministry supervisor and children's minister extraordinaire; Beeson Divinity School, for introducing me to the Apostles' Creed; Denise George, for teaching me about the writing life; Zach and Hilary Broughton, great friends and guinea pigs for this project; Sarah Joy Freese, my agent at WordServe Literary; Keren Baltzer, my editor at FaithWords; and most important, Jamie Thornton, my beautiful bride, who is by my side for all the adventures of family, ministry, and life.

Notes

INTRODUCTION

1. Deuteronomy 6:4–9. Unless otherwise noted, the NRSV is used throughout this work.

2. Voddie Baucham, Jr., *Family Driven Faith: Doing What It Takes to Raise Sons and Daughters Who Walk with God* (Wheaton: Crossway, 2011), 9, emphasis added.

3. J. Ligon Duncan III and Terry L. Johnson, "A Call to Family Worship," in *Give Praise to God: A Vision for Reforming Worship* (Phillipsburg: P&R Publishing, 2003), 320.

4. "Parents Accept Responsibility for Their Child's Spiritual Development but Struggle with Effectiveness," *Barna*, May 6, 2003, https://www.barna.com/research/parents-accept -responsibility-for-their-childs-spiritual-development-but -struggle-with-effectiveness/.

5. Tedd Tripp and Margy Tripp, *Instructing a Child's Heart* (Wapwallopen: Shepherd Press, 2008), 10.

6. Kevin J. Vanhoozer and Owen Strachan, *The Pastor as Public Theologian* (Grand Rapids: Baker Academic, 2015), 1.

7. Ibid., 4.

8. Kevin J. Vanhoozer, *Faith Speaking Understanding: Performing the Drama of Doctrine* (Louisville: Westminster John Knox, 2014), 5.

9. Mark 12:30.

10. See also Stephen J. Nichols and Ned Bustard, *Reformation ABCs: The People, Places, and Things of the Reformation— from A to Z* (Wheaton: Crossway, 2017).

11. Vanhoozer, *Faith Speaking Understanding*, 26.

12. There are a number of insightful book-length treatments of family worship, including Joel R. Beeke, *Family Worship* (Grand Rapids: Reformation Heritage, 2009); Jason Helopoulos, *A Neglected Grace: Family Worship in the Christian Home* (Fearn, Scotland: Christian Focus, 2013); Terry L. Johnson, *The Family Worship Book: A Resource Book for Family Devotions* (Fearn, Scotland: Christian Focus, 2005); and Donald S. Whitney, *Family Worship* (Wheaton: Crossway, 2016). Another very helpful and more concise work is Duncan and Johnson, "A Call to Family Worship," 317–38.

13. Baucham, *Family Driven Faith*, 102–4.

14. Peter R. Schemm, Jr., "Habits of a Gospel-Centered Household," in *Trained in the Fear of God: Family Ministry in Theological, Historical, and Practical Perspective* (Grand Rapids: Kregel Academic, 2011), 187.

15. Psalm 119:9–11.

16. Michael F. Bird, *What Christians Ought to Believe: An Introduction to Christian Doctrine Through the Apostles' Creed* (Grand Rapids: Zondervan, 2016), 13, rightly says, "The Apostles' Creed is probably the best syllabus ever devised for teaching basic Christian beliefs." Additionally, Schemm, "Habits of a Gospel-Centered Household," 180, reminds us

that the Creed is beneficial for those who presently believe and for those who do not yet possess genuine faith. The Creed both *prepares* children for faith and *sustains* and *deepens* faith.

17. This is the version of the Creed provided in Alister E. McGrath, *"I Believe": Exploring the Apostles' Creed* (Downers Grove: IVP, 1991).

18. Ibid., 14.

19. Bird, *What Christians Ought to Believe,* 37.

20. Karl Barth, *The Faith of the Church: A Commentary on the Apostles' Creed According to Calvin's Catechism*, trans. Gabriel Vahanian (Eugene: Wipf & Stock, 2006), 97.

CHAPTER 1

1. Augustine, *Confessions*, trans. Henry Chadwick (Oxford: Oxford University Press, 1991), 1.7.

2. Proverbs 22:6.

3. A. W. Tozer, *The Knowledge of the Holy* (New York: HarperOne, 1961), 1.

4. Ibid., 1–2.

5. John Calvin, *Institutes of the Christian Religion*, trans. F. L. Battles (Louisville: Westminster John Knox, 1960), 1.4.1.

6. 2 Peter 1:21; John 1:18.

7. Barth, *The Faith of the Church*, 40.

8. Deuteronomy 6:4 ESV.

9. Mark 12:29–30 ESV.

10. 1 Corinthians 8:5–6. See also Ephesians 4:6; 1 Timothy 2:5.

11. Matthew 6:9–10.

12. Titus 2:13. See also John 1:1; 2 Peter 1:1.

13. See also the end of Matthew's Gospel. The early church consistently viewed this passage as the most unmistakable affirmation of the Spirit's deity.

14. Following Thomas C. Oden, *Classic Christianity: A Systematic Theology* (New York: HarperOne, 2009), 108.

15. Wayne Grudem, *Systematic Theology: An Introduction to Biblical Doctrine* (Grand Rapids: Zondervan, 1994), 226.

16. Based on the Latin shield in Oden, *Classic Christianity*, 121.

17. C. S. Lewis, *Mere Christianity* (New York: HarperCollins, 1952), 163.

18. Ephesians 3:14–15.

19. Psalm 147:4.

20. Calvin, *Institutes* 1.11.1.

21. J. I. Packer, *Knowing God* (Downers Grove: IVP, 1973), 206–7.

22. Ephesians 2:18, 3:12.

23. Matthew 7:7–11.

24. Hebrews 12:10.

25. C. S. Lewis, *The Problem of Pain*, in *The Complete C. S. Lewis Signature Classics* (New York: HarperCollins, 2002), 385.

26. Hebrews 12:11.

27. Justo L. González, *The Apostles' Creed for Today* (Louisville: Westminster John Knox, 2007), 17.

28. John 1:14 KJV; Colossians 1:15.

29. See, for example, John 1:1–4.

30. Gerald Bray, *God Is Love: A Biblical and Systematic Theology* (Wheaton: Crossway, 2012), 116.

31. Grudem, *Systematic Theology*, 180.

32. 2 Timothy 2:13.

33. McGrath, *"I Believe,"* 29.

34. Psalm 90:2. See also Psalm 102:25–27.

35. C. S. Lewis, *The Four Loves* (New York: Harcourt, 1960; repr., 1991), 127, emphasis added.

36. Christian George, *Godology* (Chicago: Moody, 2009), 39.

37. John 1:3. For similar affirmations, see 1 Corinthians 8:6; Colossians 1:16.

38. Genesis 1:2 ESV; Psalm 104:30.

39. Lewis, *The Problem of Pain*, 429–30.

40. Calvin, *Institutes* 1.14.20.

41. Psalm 19:1.

42. Genesis 1:26.

43. Genesis 1:26–27.

44. Throughout the centuries, a variety of interpretations of the phrase "image of God" have been suggested. Probably the dominant Western interpretation has been that the image refers to the rational nature of human beings. Another common view is that the image refers to humanity's dominion over the earth: we resemble God in our respect, protection, and care for creation. The best interpretation is the one that understands the image as referring to "human life in relationship with God and with the other creatures" (Daniel L. Migliore, *Faith Seeking Understanding: An Introduction to Christian Theology*, 3rd ed. [Grand Rapids: William B. Eerdmans, 2014], 143–45). Human beings are created for life in relationships that resemble God's own life in relationship; we are created to reflect the love of the triune God, and only in this will we find our true identity, sense of belonging, and purpose.

45. Genesis 3:1–24.

46. Romans 5:12; Ephesians 2:1–3. We will explore this idea in more detail in the next chapter.

47. Gerald Bray, *The Faith We Confess: An Exposition of the Thirty-Nine Articles* (London: Latimer Trust, 2009), 68.

48. Psalm 139:7–10; Jeremiah 23:24.

49. Grudem, *Systematic Theology*, 175.

50. Calvin, *Institutes* 1.16.3, emphasis added.

CHAPTER 2

1. Genesis 2:17.

2. Ephesians 2:3.

3. Augustine, *Confessions* 1.7.

4. J. I. Packer, *Concise Theology* (Wheaton: Tyndale, 1993), 83, emphasis added.

5. I have borrowed this illustration from Bruce A. Ware, *Big Truths for Young Hearts: Teaching and Learning the Greatness of God* (Wheaton: Crossway, 2009), 96.

6. Romans 1:25. Anselm of Canterbury, *The Major Works*, eds. Brian Davies and G. R. Evans (Oxford: Oxford University Press, 1998), 283, writes, "If an angel or a man were always to render to God what he owes, he would never sin.... To sin is nothing other than not to give God what is owed to him." What is owed to God is worship, the surrender of the entire life to him.

7. Matthew 1:21.

8. J. I. Packer, *Affirming the Apostles' Creed* (Wheaton: Crossway, 2008), 60.

9. Oden, *Classic Christianity*, 248.

10. Bray, *God Is Love*, 191.

11. Hebrews 1:1–3.

12. John 1:1–3.

13. Genesis 2:7.

14. Psalm 71:15–16.

15. Deuteronomy 6:4.

16. See also, e.g., Luke 2:11; Philippians 2:9–11; Colossians 2:6.

17. One of the most exhaustive studies of this subject is Larry W. Hurtado, *Lord Jesus Christ: Devotion to Jesus in Earliest Christianity* (Grand Rapids: William B. Eerdmans, 2003).

18. On the ministry of Jesus leading up to the cross, see Bird, *What Christians Ought to Believe*, 85–97.

19. Romans 1:4 NIV.

20. Barth, *The Faith of the Church*, 75.

21. González, *The Apostles' Creed for Today*, 32–33.

22. Barth, *The Faith of the Church*, 54.

23. We first meet Gabriel in Daniel 8–9. He is a heavenly messenger, God's personal servant.

24. Barth, *The Faith of the Church*, 84.

25. Hebrews 4:15.

26. Luke 2:52; John 11:35; Matthew 4:1–11.

27. Isaiah 7:14.

28. The classic work on the virginal conception is J. Gresham Machen, *The Virgin Birth of Christ* (New York: Harper & Row, 1930).

29. Migliore, *Faith Seeking Understanding*, 181.

30. C. S. Lewis, *The Magician's Nephew* (New York: HarperCollins, 1955), 154.

31. 1 Timothy 2:5 ESV.

32. Here I am heavily indebted to Thomas F. Torrance, *Incarnation: The Person and Life of Christ*, ed. Robert T. Walker (Downers Grove: IVP Academic, 2008).

CHAPTER 3

1. Leon Morris, *The Atonement: Its Meaning and Significance* (Downers Grove: IVP Academic, 1983), 203–4.

2. Ephesians 1:7.

3. For parents who would like to learn more about the terms "redemption" and "justification," I highly recommend John Stott, *The Cross of Christ*, 20th Anniversary ed. (Downers Grove: IVP, 2006). There are numerous helpful works on the cross, though Stott's book remains one of the best. See especially the chapter "The Salvation of Sinners."

4. Romans 5:9.

5. Thomas F. Torrance, *Atonement: The Person and Work of Christ*, ed. Robert T. Walker (Downers Grove: IVP Academic, 2009), 22.

6. Bird, *What Christians Ought to Believe*, 120.

7. Matthew 27:33; Mark 15:21; John 19:17.

8. Mark 15:21.

9. Here I follow McGrath, *"I Believe,"* 59–60.

10. Cited in Martin Hengel, *Crucifixion*, trans. John Bowden (Philadelphia: Fortress Press, 1977), 25. This remains the standard work on crucifixion in the ancient world.

11. Luke 23:46.

12. González, *The Apostles' Creed for Today*, 42.

13. McGrath, *"I Believe,"* 63.

14. Bird, *What Christians Ought to Believe*, 67.

15. J. I. Packer and Mark Dever, *In My Place Condemned He Stood: Celebrating the Glory of the Atonement* (Wheaton: Crossway, 2007), 35.

16. Romans 6:23.

17. Stott, *The Cross of Christ*, 157–58.

18. Ibid., 137.

19. Hebrews 9:22.

20. Hebrews 10:4.

21. Morris, *The Atonement*, 63.

22. Torrance, *Atonement*, 9.

23. Romans 3:25; Hebrews 2:17; 1 John 2:2; 4:10 ESV.

24. Packer and Dever, *In My Place Condemned He Stood*, 77.

25. Sid Fleischman, *The Whipping Boy* (New York: Scholastic, 1986), 2.

26. Ibid.

27. Philippians 2:7–8.

28. Barth, *The Faith of the Church*, 90, points out the cohesion we need in our churches: "There is no absolute distinction between the message of Good Friday and that of Easter. For Easter is understood only through Good Friday, and Good Friday only in Easter."

29. This is one way to read 1 Peter 3:18–20 and Ephesians 4:8–10. The belief that Christ spent the interval between his crucifixion

and resurrection in the underworld was a commonplace
of Christian teaching from the earliest days. See J.N.D.
Kelly, *Early Christian Creeds*, 3rd ed. (London: Continuum
International, 1972), 379. The view I mention here is discussed
further in Bird, *What Christians Ought to Believe*, 143–50.

30. Torrance, *Atonement*, 214, emphasis in original.

31. The story is told in Charles Haddon Spurgeon, *C. H. Spurgeon
Autobiography: The Early Years, 1834–1859* (Edinburgh;
Carlisle: Banner of Truth, 1962), 87–88.

CHAPTER 4

1. Revelation 21:1.

2. Acts 1:3.

3. Josephus, *Jewish Antiquities* 4.8.15.

4. Acts 1:8.

5. Acts 1:9–11.

6. Acts 9:3–5; Revelation 1:13; Ephesians 1:20; Colossians 3:1;
   Hebrews 1:3; 1 Peter 3:22.

7. Hebrews 1:13.

8. McGrath, *"I Believe,"* 74.

9. Ephesians 1:21.

10. Barth, *The Faith of the Church*, 111, writes, "The difference
    between the Church and the world is that in the Church the Lord
    of the world is acknowledged and confessed, whereas in the
    world he is still ignored. But the same Lord rules over both."

11. Torrance, *Atonement*, 287: "As the incarnation is the meeting of
    man and God in man's place, so the ascension is the meeting of
    man and God in God's place."

12. Romans 8:34; Hebrews 7:25; Hebrews 9:24; 1 John 2:1.

13. Calvin, *Institutes* 2.16.16.

14. Bray, *God Is Love*, 598. Bird, *What Christians Ought to Believe*, 168, rightly notes, "This intercession should not be conceived of as Jesus constantly requesting *a reluctant Father* to be merciful."

15. Luke 24:40; John 20:20.

16. Oden, *Classic Christianity*, 485, says that Jesus took into the Father's presence "the evidence of atonement—his own body!"

17. Acts 1:11.

18. Migliore, *Faith Seeking Understanding*, 347, writes, "Eschatology, or the doctrine of the last things, is reflection on the Christian hope for the completion of human life in perfect fellowship with God and others and for the consummation of God's purposes for all creation."

19. Acts 1:7.

20. Matthew 7:15.

21. Actually, there are some helpful commentaries and other works. I suggest, in particular, the Revelation commentaries by G. K. Beale and Vern Poythress. For a treatment of the millennium, see *Three Views on the Millennium and Beyond* in the Counterpoints series, published by Zondervan. I find the amillennial position to be most consistent with the biblical teaching. For an excellent explanation of this view, see Sam Storms, *Kingdom Come: The Amillennial Alternative* (Mentor, 2012).

22. James 4:14.

23. Hebrews 9:27.

24. Here I prefer the ESV.

25. Barth, *The Faith of the Church*, 118.

26. Genesis 2:7.

27. Cited in Migliore, *Faith Seeking Understanding*, 364.

28. Philippians 1:23.

29. Christ's resurrection body was both *like* and *unlike* his pre-resurrection body. His disciples still recognized him. He ate fish. But he could disappear and reappear at will. Christ establishes the pattern for us; thus, Oden, *Classic Christianity*, 792, is correct when he says, "The glorified body is not a different body, but *a different form of the same body*" (emphasis added).

30. See also 1 Corinthians 15:35–54; Philippians 3:21.

31. The writer of Revelation tells us that on planet heaven there will be no more sea (verse 1). This is not to be taken literally; the sea is a symbol of chaos and evil. The removal of the sea means the removal of all challenges to God's order; it means the new creation will be a place of peace and stability. Verses 2–3 indicate that it will also be a place of great intimacy. The new Jerusalem is not a brick-and-mortar city; the city represents fellowship with God, uninterrupted communion with our Creator. Our fellowship with God will never again be hindered by sin.

32. John 11:25.

33. Genesis 6–9.

34. 2 Peter 3:7.

35. Douglas Wilson, *Heaven Misplaced: Christ's Kingdom on Earth* (Moscow, Idaho: Canon Press, 2008), 27.

36. N. T. Wright, *Surprised by Hope: Rethinking Heaven, the Resurrection, and the Mission of the Church* (New York: HarperOne, 2008), 211–12. For those interested in reading more on bodily resurrection and the new creation, I highly recommend this book by Wright.

37. C. S. Lewis, *Miracles*, in *The Complete C. S. Lewis Signature Classics* (New York: HarperCollins, 2002), 291.

38. C. S. Lewis, *The Last Battle* (New York: HarperCollins, 1956), 196, emphasis added.

CHAPTER 5

1. Acts 2:17, quoting from Joel 2:28–32.

2. Bird, *What Christians Ought to Believe*, 182.

3. This, of course, is an imperfect analogy. For example, a personal trainer stands *beside* us, while the Holy Spirit lives *within* us.

4. Christopher R. J. Holmes, *The Holy Spirit* (Grand Rapids: Zondervan, 2015), 22. Holmes goes so far as to say, "The *only content* of the Holy Spirit is Jesus" (157, emphasis added). The self-effacing ministry of the Spirit is evident in John 14:26, and especially in John 16:13–14.

5. J. I. Packer, *Keep in Step with the Spirit* (Grand Rapids: Baker Books, 2005), 57, emphasis in original.

6. Ibid.

7. Ibid.

8. Acts 5:3–4.

9. Grudem, *Systematic Theology*, 237.

10. Ephesians 4:30.

11. A more detailed discussion of the personhood of the Spirit is provided in Graham A. Cole, *He Who Gives Life: The Doctrine of the Holy Spirit* (Wheaton: Crossway, 2007), 65–72.

12. Genesis 1:2 ESV.

13. Numbers 27:8; Ezekiel 2:2, 3:24; Micah 3:8. For more on the role of the Spirit in the Old Testament, see Migliore, *Faith*

Seeking Understanding, 235–36. For a helpful treatment of the question, "Were Old Testament Believers Regenerate?" see Cole, *He Who Gives Life*, 143–45.

14. Matthew 3:16; Mark 1:10; Luke 3:22; John 1:32.

15. ESV, emphasis added.

16. John 14:16–17.

17. See the discussion of original sin in Chapter 2.

18. Romans 8:8.

19. John 6:63; Romans 8:10–11; 2 Corinthians 3:6.

20. In the words of Ezekiel 36:26: "A new heart I will give you, and a new spirit I will put within you; and I will remove from your body the heart of stone and give you a heart of flesh."

21. Cited in Migliore, *Faith Seeking Understanding*, 232.

22. Calvin, *Institutes* 3.1.1.

23. Ephesians 2:1.

24. Calvin, *Institutes* 3.2.7, emphasis added.

25. Barth, *The Faith of the Church*, 130, says, "Being God, his contact with us means a complete change. Where the Holy Spirit is, there we cannot remain as we are."

26. 2 Corinthians 5:17.

27. Augustine, *Confessions* 8.6.

28. 2 Corinthians 5:17.

29. Calvin, *Institutes* 3.3.11.

30. For a satirical take on this, see "Woman Stretching During Altar Call Accidentally Accepts Christ," *The Babylon Bee*, June 12, 2017, http://babylonbee.com/news/woman-stretching-altar-call-accidentally-accepts-christ/.

31. Calvin, *Institutes* 3.2.7.

32. Romans 10:9, emphasis added.

33. To be clear: These things do not *establish* fellowship with God; but they are *evidences* of true fellowship with God. On this subject, a great place to camp out for a while is 1 John. John announces the purpose of his first letter as follows: "I write these things to you who believe in the name of the Son of God, *so that you may know that you have eternal life*" (1 John 5:13, emphasis added). First John is about assurance. Can we be certain about our spiritual condition? John's answer is, "Yes!" Throughout the letter, he provides a series of tests to help us discern our spiritual status with absolute certainty. The four main tests are: (1) the authority of the apostles' teaching: do we submit to the teaching of Scripture? (2) the identity of Jesus: what do we believe about Jesus Christ? (3) the seriousness of sin: how do we regard sin? and (4) the necessity of love: do we display Christian love?

34. An excellent resource on this subject is Timothy Ward, *Words of Life: Scripture as the Living and Active Word of God* (Downers Grove: IVP, 2009). Ward writes, "There are three primary actions of the Holy Spirit with regard to Scripture. First, he is the agent of God's *authoring* of Scripture. It was through him that God gave the words that the writers of the Bible wrote. Second, because the Spirit is himself the living God, he also *preserves* Scripture providentially from one generation to the next. Third, in the present he is the one who opens minds to *comprehend* and hearts to *trust* what God says in Scripture" (78–79, emphasis in original).

35. 2 Peter 1:21. See also 2 Timothy 3:16, though the NRSV is misleading here ("All scripture is inspired by God"). The ESV is better. The main thrust of the verse is that the words of Scripture have their origin in God: "All Scripture is *breathed out* by God."

36. And especially in our reception of the gospel. See John 16:13; 1 Corinthians 2:6–16; 1 Thessalonians 1:4–5.

37. Calvin, *Institutes* 1.7.4

38. Acts 8:29; see also Acts 13:2, 16:6–7.

39. 1 John 4:1.

40. This is a summary of the excellent discussion in Bray, *God Is Love*, 63–65. See also Cole, *He Who Gives Life*, 273–76.

41. Bray, *God Is Love*, 65, emphasis added.

42. Barth, *The Faith of the Church*, 132–33.

43. Ephesians 2:2.

44. Packer, *Keep in Step with the Spirit*, 81.

45. Philippians 2:12–13, emphasis added.

46. One of the best works on habits of holiness is Donald S. Whitney, *Spiritual Disciplines for the Christian Life* (Colorado Springs: NavPress, 1991).

47. Galatians 5:22–23.

48. McGrath, *"I Believe,"* 86.

49. 1 Peter 4:10–11.

50. Acts 1:8.

51. See, for example, Acts 2:4, 4:8, and 7:55.

52. See, for example, 1 Thessalonians 1:5.

53. C. S. Lewis, *The Voyage of the Dawn Treader* (New York: HarperCollins, 1952), 108.

54. Ibid.

55. Ibid., 110.

56. C. S. Lewis, *The Lion, the Witch and the Wardrobe* (New York: HarperCollins, 1950), 167–68.

CHAPTER 6

1. Dietrich Bonhoeffer, *Life Together* (New York: Harper & Row, 1954), 19.

2. On this note, see the excellent work of Sherry Turkle, *Reclaiming Conversation: The Power of Talk in a Digital Age* (New York: Penguin, 2016).

3. Josh Packard, *Church Refugees* (Loveland: Group Publishing, 2015), 13. See also George Barna and David Kinnaman, eds., *Churchless* (Carol Stream: Tyndale Momentum, 2016).

4. Bird, *What Christians Ought to Believe*, 194, writes, "We are Christians only if we are churchians." Or as Augustine puts it, "He cannot have God for his father who has not the church for his mother."

5. Edmund P. Clowney, *The Church* (Downers Grove: InterVarsity, 1995), 79, says, "It is union with God that creates the unity of God's people."

6. Ephesians 4:4–6.

7. Torrance, *Atonement*, 383.

8. Genesis 11:4.

9. See, for example, Acts 2:42–47; 4:12, 32–37.

10. Torrance, *Atonement*, 382.

11. Exodus 3:5.

12. James 1:27.

13. We must be ever watchful here. According to psychology researcher Judith Rich Harris, by middle childhood already our kids are modeling their own behavior around their peer group's. See *The Nurture Assumption: Why Children Turn Out the Way They Do* (New York: Free Press, 2009), 165.

14. 1 Peter 2:9.

15. Revelation 5:9.

16. Romans 10:13.

17. Clowney, *The Church*, 77.

18. 1 Corinthians 15:3–4.

19. Bird, *What Christians Ought to Believe*, 204.

20. Gregg R. Allison, *Sojourners and Strangers: The Doctrine of the Church* (Wheaton: Crossway, 2012), 29.

21. My three questions correspond to the historical marks of the true church that have been identified since the time of the Protestant Reformation. The Lutheran statement of faith known as the Augsburg Confession defines the church as "the congregation of saints in which the gospel is rightly taught and the Sacraments rightly administered." Later confessions add a third mark: the exercise of church discipline. This is not to suggest, however, that these are the *only* marks of the church. For more on this subject, see Mark Dever, *Nine Marks of a Healthy Church*, 3rd ed. (Wheaton: Crossway, 2013); Mark Dever, *What Is a Healthy Church?* (Wheaton: Crossway, 2007).

22. For the qualifications and responsibilities of elders, see Acts 20:17–38; 1 Timothy 3:1–7, 5:17–25; Titus 1:5–9; James 5:13–16; 1 Peter 5:1–5. Deacons assist the elders in the work of ministry (1 Timothy 3:8–13).

23. 2 Timothy 4:2–3 ESV.

24. Here I lean heavily on the work of John and Noel Piper, "The Family: Together in God's Presence," *Desiring God*, January 1, 1995, http://www.desiringgod.org/articles/the-family-together -in-gods-presence. In this excellent article, the Pipers explain why parents should bring their children to corporate worship rather than send them off to children's church. In the final part of the article, Noel Piper offers a number of practical

suggestions regarding how to help children remain focused during worship.

25. Ibid.

26. Ephesians 6:1.

27. John and Noel Piper, "The Family: Together in God's Presence."

28. Matthew 28:18–19.

29. Calvin, *Institutes* 4.1.9.

30. On discipline, see especially Matthew 18:15–20.

31. See, for example, Acts 9:2.

32. Bonhoeffer, *Life Together*, 107.

33. David McCullough, *The Wright Brothers* (New York: Simon & Schuster, 2016).

About the Author

DILLON T. THORNTON (PhD in New Testament, University of Otago) has nearly two decades of diverse ministry experience. He has shepherded churches in Alabama, Colorado, and New Zealand. Presently, he serves as the senior pastor of Faith Community Church (EPC) in Seminole, Florida. Dillon is a fellow of the Center for Pastor Theologians, a highly regarded organization of local church pastors who also serve as writing theologians for the broader Christian community. In his writing, preaching, teaching, and other aspects of pastoral work, Dillon seeks to equip people of all ages to love Christ with their whole hearts, think Christianly about the world and everything in it, and live faithfully by displaying the beautiful truth of the gospel in every sphere of life. In his spare time, Dillon does CrossFit, drinks far too much coffee, reads C. S. Lewis, and watches adventure movies. He and his wife, Jamie, have two energetic boys, Aidan and Cullen.